# Cloud Charts

## Trading success

with the

## Ichimoku technique

## David Linton

Updata plc
Updata House
Old York Road
London
SW18 1TG
Great Britain

Tel: +44 (0)20 8874 4747
Fax: +44 (0)20 8874 3931
Email: enquiries@updata.co.uk
Website: www.updata.co.uk

First published in Great Britain in 2010 by Updata plc

ISBN 978-0-9565171-0-4

*British Library Cataloguing in Publication Data*
A CIP catalogue record for this book can be obtained from the British Library.

Printed and bound by Green-On, Tunbridge Wells, England.

# About the Author

**David Linton MFTA**

David Linton was born and raised near Melbourne, Australia and studied engineering at King's College, University of London in the United Kingdom. After graduating he dealt in Traded Options on the London Stock Exchange and developed computer software for analysing price behaviour. In 1991, David founded Updata plc, based in London, where he is Chief Executive Officer. Professional traders and analysts now use Updata in over forty countries around the world.

David is a well known commentator on financial markets in the UK. He has appeared on BBC television, ITN News, Bloomberg and CNBC finance channels and has written for The Mail on Sunday, Shares Magazine and the Investors Chronicle. He has taught Technical Analysis to thousands of traders and investors in Europe over the last two decades with numerous financial institutions employing him to teach and train their trading teams.

He is a member of the UK Society of Technical Analysis (STA) where he teaches the Ichimoku technique as part of the STA Diploma Course and is a holder of the MSTA designation. He is a member of the Association of American Professional Technical Analysts (AAPTA) and was awarded the Master Financial Technical Analyst (MFTA) qualification by the International Federation of Technical Analysts (IFTA) for his paper on the Optimisation of Trailing Stop-losses in 2008.

David lives in London and his interests include skiing and yachting.

# Contents

# Preface

This book represents a stage in a long journey to master the behaviour of financial markets. There are a lot of people who have impacted me along the way. This started out, for me, as a teenager when I was almost obsessed with probabilities and outcomes of all things financial. As a student in the early 1980s I would study the share pages of the Financial Times in London noting all the stocks that had jumped in price the previous day. I was fascinated to understand how a share price could suddenly leap and wanted to know how it was possible to identify such moves beforehand.

My first foray into buying shares involved reading the share tips in the weekend newspapers and ringing a stockbroker first thing on a Monday morning, buying small amounts of all of them. It seemed perfectly logical to me that they would go up because someone 'in the know' said they would and everyone reading what I was reading would be buyers too. I would give my well spoken broker my list of shares to buy, a few hundred pounds in each, while he would leave me in no doubt with his sighs that I was 'small fry'. In those days a two week account period operated. If you bought shares at the start of the account, you would have two weeks before you would have to send a cheque to your broker to pay for them. If you sold before the end of the account period and made a profit you would receive a cheque from your stockbroker for how much you had made less their commissions and stamp duty.

The first time I did this I received a cheque for over £300, and it struck me that this was the easiest way to make money in the world. I would buy shares each fortnight on Monday morning and sell them at the end of the account period on the Friday afternoon the following week. Just as I was starting to get used to the idea of receiving a cheque from my stockbroker each fortnight, something almost inconceivable to me, happened. Stocks had fallen heavily at the end of the account period one Friday and I had suffered a loss. Instead of receiving my cheque in the mail the following week, I got a statement of account that informed me that I would need to send a cheque to the broker. This would cover the difference between the prices I sold at a few days earlier and those I bought at, almost a couple of weeks beforehand as well as the commission and tax on the transactions. I had to sell the shares as I could not afford to purchase them outright, and suddenly, the idea that I would have to send a cheque for £600 pounds, almost all I had made in the proceeding weeks, and have nothing for it made me feel sick.

I remained in a state of disbelief for weeks. How could every one of the shares that were tipped to go up, do exactly the reverse and fall? They were all great companies. I had researched them in order to decide on my investment weightings. I knew their products and the companies were, indeed, undervalued as the press had pointed out. It made no sense to me that their prices fell and as the pain of the loss had subsided, I returned to watching the prices in the paper each day with an increasing resolve to profit from such moves while avoiding painful failures.

In trying to get to the bottom of my failure I started researching the idea of 'sentiment'. This was the word that was coming up in the papers as to why the markets had fallen over the period I lost money. In fact the stock market was recovering and most of the stocks I had had to sell were now higher than the prices I had bought them at. I began to realise that the direction in which the stock market as a whole moved could have as much of an impact, or bigger, on the stocks you chose to buy. I visited libraries and bookshops looking for books on this idea of sentiment and stumbled on the subject of Technical Analysis. There was very little written about it but eventually I found *Technical Analysis of the Futures Markets* by John Murphy and from that moment on I was convinced I had found the most effective way to analyse financial markets. I owe John Murphy, who I have since met a few times, thanks for this initial enlightenment.

Around this time I made a friend at college, Nick Gabriel who had a similar interest in financial markets. He and I would discuss the markets for hours on end and eventually we agreed to trade together. By then he had graduated and became an accountant and I was in my final year of study so we were both pretty busy. Despite this, we decided to trade the more exciting and leveraged London Traded Options market. We became particularly active and our broker was paying more and more attention to our dealings. I would always have the FT on me and in lectures would listen to the 'Share Check' with an ear piece on my personal radio. I would often sneak out at the back of the room and run to a payphone to deal. Nick and I had a system of calling an answerphone to leave messages for each other. We would call in and retrieve these first before dealing and leave messages to what each of us was doing with our trading account. Miraculously we never did the same thing individually at the same time.

Our strategy for buying and selling was based on work we had done with some basic software on an Amstrad PCW. The screen was monochrome and the print outs were poor but at the time we felt we had a real edge in the market and we began to trade bigger amounts. I recall in early 1987 that we managed to turn £100 on a first trade into £10,000 in the space of weeks on options that were rocketing. It was a very exciting time. But we had our failures too and after several months we had little to show from all our efforts. By the late summer of 1987 we decided to take a break from trading. It seemed the markets were harder to read and very inflated, and committing time to trading was also becoming an issue. As it happened, quite by luck, we were not at all involved in the stock market crash of October 1987. Even now it is hard to conceive prices across the board halving in a day or two. I was stunned as I read the dramatic headlines in the FT. I remember feeling an enormous sense of relief that I was not involved in the '87 crash, but also could not help thinking I had missed a 'once in a lifetime' opportunity of making a fortune with 'out of the money' put options.

Nick and I returned to looking at markets after I graduated and started to develop software programs which would be more powerful than anything we had come across. One of the biggest hassles of running this sort of analysis software in those days was entering all the data. Typing in yesterday's share prices, one by one, from the paper each day was such a tiring exercise, that by the time you had finished you had virtually no appetite left for conducting the analysis. Added to this frustration was the knowledge that you were looking at charts of prices that were at least a day old.

In the late 1980s most private investors in the UK looked at share prices on a service called Teletext. This was a text based scrolling page service operated with a remote control on a television. It contained news headlines, sport, travel information, last minute holiday offers and, most of all, share prices that were updated several times a day. Soon circuit cards became available for personal computers where, by plugging in a TV aerial, you could view Teletext pages on your screen. We soon realised that once these pages were on a computer screen, there must be a way to strip the prices from the pages and store them. Suddenly we had computerised charts that were updated several times a day and we could see our simple program had commercial potential. I came up with the name Updata because it took so much work out of updating prices to draw charts and we set up a business. After a few months of struggling to sell our system, Nick decided to leave the company and I took over Updata and its debts.

Having spoken to so many potential prospects for the Updata program, I was lucky enough to meet Ian Rodgers who had worked in the City for many years. He and a couple of friends agreed to back the company and Ian became a mentor in the early years of getting Updata off the ground. Without all of his hours of dedication and support, along with a deep personal interest to see me succeed, Updata would be nothing like the business it has become today. For that I will always be grateful to him. In the early years the company benefited from numerous supporters. Patrick Littlehales, a stockbroker and one of our first clients and backers helped to get our software running in more demanding trading environments. Theo van Dort, a veteran in accounting software was a valuable advisor behind the scenes. Sadly he died a few years ago and I regularly miss him.

The first Updata software product was ahead of its time, with a number of firsts for investment software in the UK. Besides leading in the updating of the software, you could use a mouse to draw trend lines, which was quite something for an MS DOS program. It had the first trailing stop-losses, which were also mouse driven, and we strived to beat competing UK companies such as Fairshares and Indexia, businesses that Updata later acquired. We were the first to move to Microsoft Windows which was considered a risk at the time. We also benefited from being the first to sign a deal with Teletext and other providers of broadcast real-time data. These days were way before it was fashionable to join an internet start-up and many people came and worked for us on low pay. People like Neil Roodyn and Stephen Onerhime spent many years with the business developing our technology.

Updata is a very different company today and we have a great team of talented people. Sami Khan, Richard Teale, Nigel Shaw, Andrew Mckendrick, Jeremy du Plessis, Hammaad Uteem and Tara Babooa have been with us for years and helped us stay at the forefront. Newer members of staff have played their part in making our business grow to the point where our customers now include most of the top financial institutions in the world across more than forty countries.

We would not have been able to make the strides we have in Technical Trading systems without the thousands of private customers over the years. Many of these people still subscribe to our products today recognising the value of paying for a system with higher capabilities than free, advertising funded services on the internet.

Our customers keep us clean by paying us direct and we work around the clock to make as many of the enhancements that they ask for, as possible.

There have been many professional clients who have influenced my work in Technical Analysis and the development of our products; Jeff Hochman at Fidelity in London, Robin Griffiths at JP Morgan Cazenove, Rob Brand at ABN Amro, Adam Sorab at CQS Management, David Sneddon at Credit Suisse, Dave Keller at Fidelity in Boston, Cyril Baudrillart at Exane BNP Paribas, Charlie Morris at HSBC, Kevin Edgeley at Caxton Europe, Axel Rudolph at Commerzbank, Alan Johnson at Mirabaud Securities, Tim Parker at PH Partners, Jean-Charles Gand at Societe Generale, Greg Morris at Stadion Money Management and Louise Yamada at LY advisors in New York. These people, and many others that I will have failed to mention, have all had an influence, often greater than they could know. Without them this book would not have been possible. Over the last few years I have delivered a series of training courses to market professionals in a number of countries and I am also grateful to them for their feedback in developing lots of the ideas in this book.

The team behind the Updata software also deserve special mention. The book would have been impossible to produce without it and the speed at which I have been able to produce the charts, annotate them and explore new ideas has constantly reminded me along the way how much of an incredible product Updata is. Sure, I am biased, but I also know a growing band of people around the world would agree. For this special thanks goes to Jeremy du Plessis, Sami Khan, Nigel Shaw and Andrew Mckendrick at Updata plc.

I would probably not be writing this book without two people in particular. Rick Bensignor, at Morgan Stanley in New York inspired my first interest in the Ichimoku technique several years ago. John Cameron, Head of Education at the UK Society of Technical Analysts encouraged me to teach the subject which, in turn, pushed me to learn as much as I could about it.

In terms of my work as a Technical Analyst, one person has influenced my knowledge to a far higher extent than anyone and I have been fortunate to work with him for several years. Jeremy du Plessis, Head of Technical Analysis is the most learned proponent of the overall subject that I have encountered. He is one of the most qualified technicians in the UK as a Fellow of the Society of Technical Analysts (FSTA) and a Chartered Market Technician (CMT), a designation widely recognised in the USA. He is probably the world's leading expert on the Point and Figure charting technique and the author of *The Definitive Guide to Point and Figure*. I have been lucky to have had Jeremy to hand over the years to correct any mistakes and misunderstandings in my work in Technical Analysis. Had it not been for working with Jeremy, you would almost certainly be reading a much lesser book here. So to him I am grateful.

There are numerous friends and colleagues to thank for their support over the years and in particular, my parents who have always provided their encouragement and never pressured me to get 'a proper job' when I spent years working to get Updata off the ground. To them and all other friends who have helped me, thank you.

# Acknowledgements

While many people lie behind the foundations of writing a book, it is the turmoil that ensues once you have started that requires you to rely heavily on people. All of the team at Updata have had to run around me or have me ignore them to some extent while I wrote this book. Jeremy du Plessis, Peter Shaw, Richard Teale and Gurpreet Rai helped with proofing the text. Charlotte Andersen and Sami Khan deserve special mention for editing, indexing and technical assistance. David Donovan, at Updata wrote a number of Updata Custom Indicators with the help of Sami Khan and assisted with back-testing the Ichimoku technique which enabled me to produce Part 3 of the book. Mariko Takahashi translated the Japanese texts I needed to produce various sections. Gemma Lofts, studying a degree in English literature, brought much needed grammatical order to the book with her editing.

There is a saying that England and America are two countries separated by the same language. The first edition of the book is written in UK English, not American English. Consequently words such as 'color' are spelt 'colour'. I apologise in advance to readers in America. I am also grateful to the late Hidenobu Sasaki for his book in Japanese on Ichimoku. If I have misinterpreted or missed anything, I am sorry, and would be grateful to be informed by anyone in Japan who has further findings on the subject.

Peter Shaw at Updata handled most of the logistics of publishing and distributing the book. Chris Steel at 521 Design, Matt Spencer at 3mil and Albert Becker at Green-On worked to an impossibly tight schedule on the design, layout and printing. It is thanks to them that this full colour book looks so good.

Finally, thanks are due to my family and friends for allowing me to shut myself away to write this book particularly for three weeks when I went away alone over Christmas 2009. My girlfriend, Barbara Graham, was also regularly neglected and patient with me throughout. Thank you so much Honey!

# Feedback

I welcome feedback at David@cloudcharts.com

All charts in the book are produced using Updata Professional. The data for many of these charts is courtesy of Bloomberg LP.

# Introduction

Every year around the end of October the International Federation of Technical Analysts (IFTA) holds its annual conference. Members from technical analysis societies around the world gather to share their experience and hear the latest ideas in presentations over the course of a few days. In 2004, it was the turn of the Asociación Española de Analistas Técnicos to host the IFTA conference in Madrid. It was a memorable event and it was great to have so many esteemed technicians in one gathering.

By nature, running a software company that covers so many bases in technical analysis and travelling the world to meet some of the best names in the business at their desks, it is rare that a conference presentation breaks new ground. But, as with reading a book, you never know what gem you will pick up buried deep within the content. One of the speakers at the Madrid conference was Rick Bensignor, who was then Chief Technical Strategist at Morgan Stanley and his presentation was about Ichimoku Kinkho Hyo charts. I had seen these 'Cloud Charts' before and heard people speak about them in other presentations, but on that November morning, Rick presented them in a way that made them understandable to many of us in the audience for the first time. That is where this started for me. As a result I am grateful to Rick Bensignor for sparking my interest in the Ichimoku technique.

Soon after Madrid, I started looking at these charts more and more and I was keen to find out as much as I could about them. The charts seemed to display a natural phenomenon in mapping the price of a financial instrument with an uncanny degree of accuracy. I wanted to know why this was, so I searched the internet only to find descriptions on their construction, which is elegantly simple as we shall see in Part 2. There was a real lack of material that explored these charts in any meaningful depth. I visited Rick in New York and met up with him at subsequent IFTA conferences in Switzerland and Egypt. I spoke with other technical analysts based in London who used them. I approached the Japanese delegates at the IFTA conferences each year in a bid to find out how they used them. Did they have any further gems of wisdom? Did they know of anyone in Japan I should speak to? I was drawing blanks. Many of the Westerners I spoke to implied that there was a bigger secret and while the Japanese analysts were always politely enthusiastic, I sensed that they also might be holding something back.

My curiosity towards Cloud Charts coincided with their increasing appearance in my work. They were becoming a regular part of my weekly commentaries on markets, and featured in my monthly reports and in presentations. I would show them in television interviews and webcasts and found myself using them to explain what was going on when sitting at trading desks with institutional clients. The UK Society of Technical Analysts (STA) asked me to speak on the subject and then invited me to prepare and present a module for the STA Diploma evening course, taught at the start of every year in London. A growing number of people were turning to me to explain the Ichimoku technique more fully. Part of me felt uncomfortable that I might not know all there was to the subject, while another side of me questioned if there was any more to it anyway.

For Christmas 2007, I flew to Tokyo with the aim of finding out as much as I could about the Ichimoku technique. Nothing quite prepares you for your first time arrival as a Westerner in Japan. If you take a ride on the subway system you are confronted with a map of spaghetti that has kanji characters all over it. Trying to find 一目均衡表 (Ichimoku in Japanese) on the spine of books in rows of shelves in the bigger book shops in Tokyo was an even bigger step. In fairness everyone was very polite and spoke English, but communication was still difficult. This was probably as a result of my poor pronunciation of Ichimoku Kinkho Hyo or my attempt at replication of the characters on a piece of paper.

Apart from finding Japanese books on Cloud Charts, I resolved to see as many market professionals as I could in Tokyo. I had four meetings with different clients on Boxing Day and each one started in virtually the same manner. The client would say to me, "So what can you tell me about these Ichimoku charts?" The person I most wanted to meet was Hidenobu Sasaki. He was the man that Japanese delegates at IFTA conferences most recommended. He had worked for a number of leading firms, won awards and had written books on finance. One of his books was on the Ichimoku technique and I had managed to obtain a copy. Despite several attempts I was unable to meet Mr Sasaki. I guess he had been hounded in Japan where Ichimoku has a big following. Sadly he died September 2008 and perhaps some Ichimoku secrets, over and above what he has published, have been lost forever.

## Lost in translation

The most preferred translated title of Sasaki's book seems to be 'Table of equilibrium at a glance' although it is sometimes referred to as 'Ichimoku balance chart' in Japan. As we will come to see these names are apt descriptions of the subject. While I do have other Japanese books that cover Cloud Charts, including a volume by Goichi Hosoda who devised the charts, Sasaki's is the best text. I will do my best to unearth it and a good deal more besides.

I feel at this point that I should emphasise some of the difficulty in taking the available information in Japanese of this Japanese technique and presenting it in English. The problem is two-fold. First the translations that I have had done, which are by no means exhaustive, vary from translator to translator when explained in English. The fact that Sasaki's book title goes by a number of titles in English is a testament to this. Ask several Japanese people to tell you what it means in English and you get a number of answers. This is only a reflection on the difficulty in conducting a literal translation from Japanese to English. So for this book I have had to do my best at reading between the lines in some areas.

The second difficulty is cultural. The variations in translations do have a common theme in the concepts and metaphors the Japanese seem to use in the subject. This Japanese descriptive style is also borne from the many warrior-like names given to the various patterns in Candlestick charts. They clearly have a rich Japanese cultural heritage. In reading Greg Morris' book on Candlestick charts he recounts the time he spent with people in Japan who had mastered the technique. In attempting to present Cloud Charts in English, I have not had the benefit of meeting a true Japanese master in the subject who could clarify uncertainties in the translation. The Ichimoku technique is much newer, consequently there are fewer experts available, and little documentation to bridge this gap. As a result, I have steered away from the Japanese names and stuck to plain English as much as possible. The basic Japanese terminology is included in the glossary at the end of this book.

In recent years so many people have asked why I haven't written this book. Professional traders ask me to explain Cloud Charts when I visit their desks. Numerous people in the world's financial centres now have Cloud Charts on their screens without much understanding of how to use them. I am approached at conferences and training. I have found myself going over it with so many people, one after another, that the time has come to write it all down.

As much as possible I have tried to make this subject understandable to someone new to the world of technical analysis. I have outlined the most useful techniques in Part 1 as an overview to the subject to help you understand how Cloud Charts are best used as an additional tool. The more experienced technical analyst may choose to gloss over these areas, but if you are looking for further information, some of the best books in technical analysis are highlighted in the Bibliography.

For some time I thought there wasn't really enough to Cloud Charts for a book. The technique itself is truly brilliant and quite straightforward. But more and more people are using clouds and asking questions. It is easy to forget that I spent a while not understanding these charts, until someone enlightened me.

Hopefully, I can do the same for you!

**David Linton**
March 2010, London

# About this book

## Part 1

The book is split into three parts. Part 1 is designed to give you enough knowledge of technical analysis in order that you may fully understand Cloud Charts, complimentary techniques and more advanced ideas. It is by no means a comprehensive guide to the whole subject. The better your understanding of technical analysis, the easier you will find understanding Cloud Charts. It should be possible to get up-and-running with using Cloud Charts from this book alone. The explanations of support and resistance, moving averages and basic Candlestick charts in these early chapters are all fairly essential to understanding Cloud Charts.

We have also covered basic technical analysis indicators in Part 1 so you may gain an understanding of how they are applied in more advanced Cloud Chart techniques outlined in Part 3. There is a chapter on Point and Figure charting as this really powerful technique often agrees with what Cloud Charts tell us about an instrument. We show the power of using Cloud Charts and Point and Figure together later in the book.

Towards the end of Part 1, stop-losses and money management are covered. While the tools shown here are not strictly technical analysis techniques they are a vital tool for any trader. There will be times where tools such as stop-losses take precedence over other techniques including Cloud Charts as we will come to see. Understanding trailing stop-losses will also be helpful when we come to explore the idea of cloud stops-losses in Part 3.

If you are already an experienced technician, you may choose to skip Part 1. But a quick revision of the subject may be useful and might uncover some things you did not fully appreciate.

## Part 2

This section of the book addresses the basics of using Cloud Charts. If you are only interested in getting to grips with the technique and using it, you could get by on this section of the book alone. The construction chapter is important to truly understand these charts and apply them as covered in Chapter 10. The chapter on time horizon is vital for maximising the value of Cloud Charts for multiple time frame analysis. Chapter 12 looks at using Cloud Charts alongside other techniques with some practical examples.

## Part 3

The final part of the book looks at some more advanced analysis ideas and trading strategies. Many of these ideas are derived from applying the standard techniques covered in Part 1 to Cloud Charts. While you can easily conduct cloud analysis from only reading Part 2, Part 3 might inspire an extra idea or two. Hopefully you will find some of the new material in this final section original and groundbreaking enough to want to apply to your own trading.

## Software and Systems

The most important thing of all with this book is to start using Cloud Charts while you are learning about them. You may already have them on the software system you use which should be enough to learn how to use them. If you want to be certain of following all the techniques covered in this book, you can download a free trial of Updata and do your own analysis on instruments of your choice. Simply type in keywords and names in the help box in the top right hand corner of the software tool bar and use them in practice as you read.

If you are a market professional, download a trial of Updata Professional at **www.updata.co.uk**

This system is Updata's flagship product used in dealing rooms in over 40 countries and seamlessly compatible with a host of professional services including Bloomberg and Reuters.

Private investors or home based can download a trial of Trader*Pro* at **www.updata.co.uk/private**

This software runs with a full list of lost cost and free services including Google Finance and Yahoo! Finance.

## CloudCharts.com

Cloud charting is still a relatively new technique and it is likely to continue to develop. For further material including reports and analysis, new Cloud Chart techniques and webcasts visit - **www.cloudcharts.com**

# Part 1 - **Understanding Technical Analysis**

---

*"I know all this has been said before, but I need to say it anyway"*

Jean-Jacques Rousseau 1712-1778

# Chapter 1 - **History**

The cloud chart technique is one of the newest forms of Technical Analysis, a subject that has been described in many ways over the years, often referred to as Charting. Technical Analysts in the US are normally called Technicians and in many parts of the world they are often colloquially known as Chartists. For many years analysts, particularly of share prices, fell into one of two camps. You were either a fundamental analyst or a technical analyst. It was rare that you used both forms of analysis as the approaches are so different.

## Fundamentals versus Technicals

Fundamental analysis is by far the most common route that investors took. This required you to analyse all the underlying information about a company such as annual accounts, trends of demand for products, news, directors' share transactions or macro economics. You name it, anything that could affect the price. It all seemed very logical but the problem with this form of analysis is that nearly all this information is already reflected in the price. So unless you have managed to spot something that very few people have it is unlikely that any information you find will help you predict where the price is going. We see this all the time when prices go down on good news because it wasn't as good as expected. Similarly the price can rise when the news isn't as bad as was feared. Good news does not necessarily make prices go up!

Fundamental analysis is essentially an analysis of value, while technical analysis studies price. Value and price are two different things. If they were the same, there would be little need for financial markets. Nothing would be overvalued or undervalued. While fundamental factors may have a bearing on prices in the long run, shorter term moves are more likely to be entirely technical. The price chart represents everything that everyone knows in the market at that time. New information may come to light in the form of news which can affect the price, but there was little chance of knowing it. The extent to which the price reacts to such an event will often be technical. The Microsoft chart below shows that in late 2007 the company had a market value of around $350 billion. Less than 18 months later the company was capitalised at less than $150 billion.

Chart 1-1: Microsoft market capitalisation over 3 years

These valuations are much more about what market participants were willing to pay than slower moving metrics such as profit and loss accounts and balance sheets. Market sentiment will have had a bigger impact than company performance on price and there are more extreme examples.

The purest form of analysis ignores all the underlying information that a fundamental analyst is likely to use. It is a study of effect rather than cause. Technicians don't necessarily care why something is happening but are instead focused on what is occurring in the share price chart. Of course for the pure fundamental analyst, this approach seems completely illogical. The technician may use a host of analysis tools and indicators which can be derived from the price history in order to assist with predicting likely future price moves. Cloud Charts are just one of these tools and we will explore the basics of technical analysis in this part of the book.

Many participants in financial markets consider technical analysis to be a relatively new subject. Technical traders rely on the charts on their screens for their trading signals and as a result it is a common misconception that the subject of Technical Analysis was born in the last few decades with the advent of personal computers. Indeed some scepticism exists over the technical approach because people still see chart analysis as a fairly new idea. Charts were in fact used in the Western world well over a century ago and the Japanese have been using them for longer still.

## Western chart history

The earliest reference to what we now know as technical analysis, was recorded by Charles Dow. Born in 1851, he was an American journalist who co-founded the Dow Jones & Company. Dow also founded the Wall Street Journal and devised the Dow Jones Index as part of his work in researching market movements. Many of his observations were recorded in the Wall Street Journal, and after his death in 1902, the then editor and two colleagues reviewed and summarised some 250 of Dow's editorials to produce what we now know as Dow Theory.

Dow Theory mapped out six basic tenets:

1. The market has three movements – primary or major trend of about a year to several years, the medium swing or intermediate reaction of 10 days to 3 months and generally retracing 33% to 66% of the major trend and the short swing or minor movement which can last from hours to weeks. These movements can all be occurring simultaneously – trends, within trends, within trends.
2. The trends have three phases – an accumulation phase with shrewd investors 'in the know' acting contrary to popular opinion, a public participation phase where the market catches on and prices move more dramatically and a distribution phase where the astute investors begin to unwind their positions.
3. The stock market discounts all news – prices quickly absorb all new information as soon as it becomes available. This was quite an admission from the editor of the leading newspaper at the time and agrees with what we now know as efficient market hypothesis.

4. Stock market averages must confirm each other – Dow also devised the Transports Average, which like the better known Dow Jones Industrials Average, survives to this day. Calculated using rail and industry stocks respectively, Dow argued that they need to confirm each other for any trend in prices to be believed. While this exact relationship is little used today, this idea probably sparked the concept of 'divergence' between price and other technical indicators. Now a mainstream idea, we will explore divergence in Part 1.
5. Trends are confirmed by volume – Dow believed that price moves accompanied by high volume represented the 'true' market view and that price moves on low volume were to be taken less seriously. This is also in line with the later ideas of confirmation and divergence noted with many technical analysis tools.
6. Trends exist until definitive signals prove that they have ended otherwise – the primary trend should be given the benefit of the doubt during secondary reversals. Here is the foundation of what we now know as 'the trend is your friend.' Cloud Charts are especially helpful in knowing when a trend has ended and we will explore this at length throughout the book.

Although Dow's original ideas form the basis of the subject of technical analysis in the West as we know it today, it is not entirely clear how heavily these techniques were being used by the trading community at the time. In his book *The Definitive Guide to Point and Figure,* Jeremy du Plessis cites textbook references in the middle of the last century pointing to the use of Point and Figure charts pre-1900.

One thing we do know, is that many books on Technical Analysis were written from the 1920s onwards. Their titles more commonly referred to 'forecasting' or 'technical methods,' and it probably wasn't until Robert Edwards and John Magee published *Technical Analysis of Stock Trends* in 1948, that the subject of Technical Analysis gained traction as a method of analysis. Edwards and Magees' seminal work is now in its ninth edition and their definition of technical analysis is still one of the most cited, even today:

> *"Technical analysis is the science of recording, usually in graphic form, the actual history of trading (meaning price changes, volumes etc) in a certain share, or commodity etc, and then deducting from that pictured history, the probable future trend."*

Contributors to the subject ever since are too numerous to mention in all. Technicians such as J. Welles Wilder Jnr introduced a raft of new indicators in his 1978 book – New Concepts in Technical Trading Systems (a title that wouldn't be out of place today). Traders around the world have his RSI indicator in a bottom window on their screens each day. In 1986, John Murphy produced Technical Analysis of the Futures Markets which was the 'must read' for anyone involved with technical analysis at the time. It became known as the 'Bible' on the subject for its shear breadth and depth of coverage. For this reason Murphy is often considered the modern father of Technical Analysis.

## Japanese chart history

Look at virtually any charting service today and you will find candle stick charts as an option. Lots of people use them as their standard chart, but few people in the Western World know how these charts were developed in Japan a few centuries ago. Japanese technical analysts point to Munehisa Homma who was renowned for having made a huge fortune trading rice in the eighteenth century. Japan had been undergoing feudal conflict internally for a couple of hundred years when sixty provinces finally emerged as one. The country had undergone a period of foreign isolation from the middle of the seventeenth century but as a unified force domestic commerce blossomed. At the end of the seventeenth century, rice trading was centralised to a national market in Osaka, the Dojima Rice Exchange, replacing a series of fragmented provincial markets. This new liquid market is probably where 'technical trading' first began. Rice futures were traded on this exchange in the early eighteenth century with well over 1,000 rice traders participating on the Osaka exchange. By the mid 1700s trading in rice futures on the exchange was nearly four times that of the physical amount of rice produced.

Munehisa Homma started trading on the Osaka rice exchange in 1750 having inherited a large family fortune including a vast rice farming operation. Homma analysed rice prices on the exchange as far back as he could to understand the psychology of the participants and trading patterns. Homma went on to produce books documenting his rice trading techniques, which are said to be the beginning of the Candlestick charting method.

We will look briefly at the construction of Candlestick charts and the most important patterns in this book as they are integral to Cloud Charts. It is interesting to note the way Japanese history is embedded in this analysis. There are literally hundreds of patterns made up of different candles representing each trading day. We will cover the main ones in Chapter 6, but here are a few below to demonstrate how mythical warrior-like names are used. Even today, when discussing Candlesticks with Japanese traders, the passion of the fight between bulls (buyers) and bears (sellers) in a sort of titanic battle comes through.

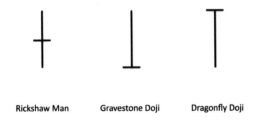

Rickshaw Man      Gravestone Doji      Dragonfly Doji

Figure 1-1: Japanese Candlesticks

While history records the commencement of the opening up of Japan after the arrival of the American commodore Matthew Perry in 1853, there is little evidence of much exchange of investment ideas until the latter half of the twentieth century. Whether the Japanese were using Dow Theory before World War II or if some westerners were already familiar with Candlesticks is little known. The fact that Japan and the West discovered and developed their own Technical Analysis techniques independently is an interesting coincidence. Analysing past prices to predict future moves was there to be uncovered.

## East meets West

In 1984 members of the Market Technicians Association (MTA) and the Nippon Technical Analysts Association (NTAA) met in southern California. As a result of this meeting, the International Federation of Technical Analysts (IFTA) was formed with the Society of Technical Analysts (STA) in London joining as well. A seminar was held in Tokyo the following year and the first annual conference was also held in Tokyo in 1988. IFTA now has 20 member countries with the conference been hosted annually in one of these countries. It is clear that Western analysts developed an interest in learning more about Japanese technical analysis techniques and the exchange truly began around this time.

In 1991 Steve Nison's book *Japanese Candlestck Charting Techniques* was published and widely accredited with introducing Candlestick charts to the Western world. In 1992 the well known technician Greg Morris, published *Candlestick Charting Explained* which is also a very good point of reference.

## History of Cloud Charts

The Ichimoku charting technique was devised by Goichi Hosoda (1898 – 1982) who worked as a journalist for the Capital Newspaper (Tokyo Shimbun) covering stock markets. He later became the paper's business editor. In 1932 Hosoda formed a team of seven people to work on the development of the Ichimoku chart. One can only imagine that this team was employed to run a series of mathematical optimisations by hand in order to arrive at the best formulae and parameters to use. In the spring of 1935, Hosoda announced the 'Sinto Tenkan Sen' (turn conversion line) and published it in the Capital Newspaper and Japan Securities Finance Journal. He is said to have written under the pseudonym 'Ichimoku Sanjin' (at a glance of a man standing on a mountain) but the more common translation of 'Ichi-moku' is 'one look. The full name of the technique Ichimoku Kinko Hyo translates as below:

Ichimoku – At one glance     Kinko – balance     Hyo – bar chart

Technical research was yet to be developed at this time and the Ichimoku charts rapidly attained enormous popularity among the Japanese finance community. Hosoda's articles were published in the leading publication Shito each week, highlighting promising stocks under the Ichimoku banner. Although the lines were simple to produce, Hosoda kept them secret until 1950 when he revealed the calculation to a group of friends on the promise that they in turn would keep the information secret for a further ten years. In 1968 Hosoda published the findings of his work titled *Ichimoku Kinko Hyo* in seven volumes.

Hosoda explained for the first time that the Ichimoku chart is composed of a Kijun-sen (Base or Standard line) a Tenkan-sen (Conversion or Turning line), Senkou Span A (Leading span A), Senkou Span B (Leading Span B) and the Chikou Span (Lagging Span). The area enclosed by the two leading spans is called the Kumo (cloud) which is the most striking part of these charts. The cloud is said to be based on the idea that time is valuable and the market moves in the direction where the equilibrium between buyers and sellers has changed. Hosoda also identified three principles: wave principle, price targets and time span principle. He argued that the point of the technique, once fully understood, was to be able to understand the exact status of the chart at a glance. The chart below shows the Cloud Chart composition. We will cover the construction and interpretation in subsequent chapters.

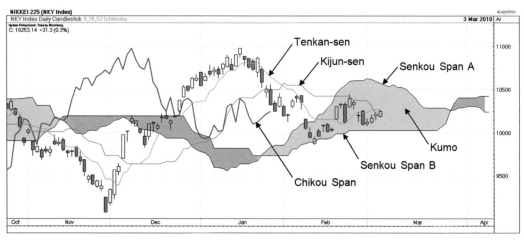

Chart 1-2: Ichimoku Chart with the Japanese names of lines

The best Japanese book on the Ichimoku technique is by Hidenobu Sasaki. It was published by Toshi Radar in 1996. The most literal translation of the title appears to be *Table of equilibrium at a glance* although it is sometimes referred to as *Study of Ichimoku Balance Chart*. It has been through many editions and won awards for several years.

However Cloud Charts have developed, they have made it on to trading screens all over the Western World. It is likely their popularity will increase, especially given the simplicity of the technique.

# Chapter 2 - **Basics of Technical Analysis**

Most of us appreciate the advantage of representing a series of numbers as a graph. In our early mathematics lessons at school we learn how to plot data on two axes to get a pictorial representation. If you run a business and enter all your sales numbers in a spreadsheet, by the end of it you are itching to drag your mouse over all the data and click the draw a chart button. Why? Because we all know that a graph helps us see things, such as trends, that we might easily miss by looking at the raw numbers alone. A picture is so much more valuable and can help you get a feel for where the data is heading. The chart below is of….well in fact it doesn't matter what it is of. You can rely on the chart alone to guide you. Where do you think the price is likely to go next?

Figure 2-1: Nationwide UK House Price Index 1991 - 2009, courtesy of Nationwide Building Society

If you do technical analysis for long enough, the chart at a first glance tells you most of what you need to know. You get a feel for what more detailed analysis is going to tell you. And the key point here is that the price chart in technical analysis is more important than any indicator you can derive from it. The basic theories, set out by Charles Dow, cited in Chapter 1 are central to understanding price behaviour.

## The trend is your friend

You have probably heard this before and it sounds obvious, but the real meaning of this adage is don't try and pick the top or the bottom. It is in our nature to want to be the clever guy who got in at the very bottom and out at the very top. No trader can consistently do this.

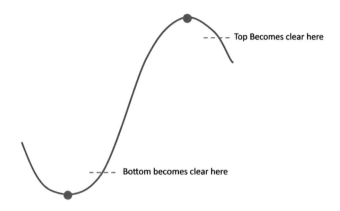

Figure 2-2: We can only know tops and bottoms retrospectively

We can only truly know a bottom or a top retrospectively. If we look at the simplified cycle above it is normally around point B, that we find ourselves looking at the low point at A and saying 'I wish I bought there.' We make a note to ourselves, that if prices hit that level again, we will buy. The price often doesn't return to these levels and the opportunity is missed. When you first find yourself saying 'I should have bought there', you probably have a buy signal. Equally, at D we look back at C and say to ourselves 'I should have sold there.' We make a little prayer for prices to go back up and make a mental promise to sell next time they are at C. Normally the new trend wins and we miss our opportunity to get out at good price levels.

Prices generally spend more time trending than they do reversing. Reversals normally occur over a relatively shorter period. Therefore being a trend follower means you will be right most of the time, but wrong at the tops and the bottoms. Whereas if you are a top and bottom picker you will be wrong all the way up the trend and down again, while you will eventually be right at the top and the bottom. Identifying trends and reversals is what technical analysis is all about and we will come to see that Cloud Charts are especially good for identifying them.

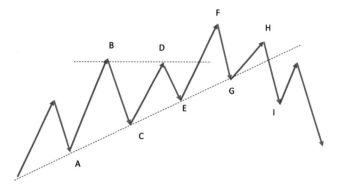

Figure 2-3: Anatomy of buyers and seller in an uptrend

## The importance of higher highs and lower lows

To get an understanding of how crowd psychology and technical analysis are closely aligned, let us walk through the diagram of price moves above. Prices are initially going up and fall back to find support of buyers coming in at A where they turn and start to rise again. From here they rise higher still until they hit a level at B where sellers come in forcing prices to fall again. The sellers persist, but at C, buyers start coming in and the price starts to rise again. At this point we know something that is simple but significant. People trading at C are now prepared to pay more for this asset than they were at A. They are not letting it fall back as far this time before they come in and buy. The sellers are being squeezed and the buyers are happy to come in at these levels. So prices start rising again, until, at D, they hit resistance, which, in this case, happens to be at the same level as B. People sold at this level last time and they are selling at the same level again. Some of these sellers will be the people who bought at B and saw prices fall and are now selling at D having promised to get out if the price got back to this level. So the pressure of the sellers at D pushes prices back down but not so far this time and at E the buyers are prepared to come in again.

It is around the point E that we start to see a trend. Buyers have been coming in at progressively higher levels, A, C and E, prepared to pay more for this asset as time elapses. After E we might expect some resistance at the same level as D (and B) with sellers coming back in, but the price breaks through to higher levels. New highs are a bullish signal to the technician and something of an anathema to the fundamental analyst. As the price goes up, the fundamentals generally become less favourable. At the point F, prices have now risen so far that people are happy to take profits and the sellers return at these levels and prices fall back to G. This is the point where we would expect some support for the price in line with what is now a visible trend in prices set by the previous lows at A, C and E.

Prices start to rise again after G and the trend is now very clear and we expect to see a new high above the level we saw at F. But this time prices don't go that high and we see a reversal at H. This is highly significant because for the first time this asset is being sold at a lower level than it was before. The buyers are not prepared to pay more and the sellers are happy to come in at lower levels. The reversal at H is not a sell signal in itself because the uptrend is still intact, but the lower high should be putting us on alert that the trend may be ending. So, after H, prices start falling. The next worrying sign is that the uptrend line (support) created by A, C, E and G is breached for the first time. This might be temporary and we could see buyers come back in at the same price level as G. They bought here last time and may well do so again. But prices continue to fall going lower than G. This is now a clear sell signal. People are not prepared to pay as much as they did before, let alone more. So we fall to the point 'I' to make a lower low where some buyers do come in. But the combination of a lower high and a lower low after a run of higher highs and higher lows tells us that this uptrend has ended.

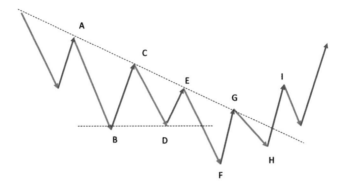

Figure 2.4: Anatomy of sellers and buyers in a downtrend

Invariably with technical analysis, the reversal applies by turning things the other way up. So the signs that a downtrend is ending is a higher low followed by a higher high.

These diagrams are of course a simplistic representation of price movement and in the real world charts are invariably more complex. As Charles Dow stipulated we will see trends within trends. Here we see a representation of the three major moves that Dow stipulated. A primary trend of a few years or more is shown with a secondary reaction of a few months retracing anywhere between a third and two thirds of the major run. Then a short term trend of a few weeks is shown. Cloud Charts are brilliant for resolving these trends with different time frames as we will come to see in Part 2. We have also highlighted the phases within a single trend that Dow identified – accumulation by shrewd investors, public participation and distribution (selling) by the astute few again.

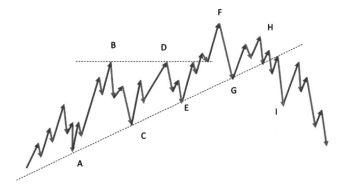

Figure 2-5: In reality price movement in markets is complex

Financial markets are highly complex. They involve millions of market participants with a vast range of time horizons representing the individual needs of billions of people. There are various cycles and trends within trends within trends. One analogy to gain an understanding of this complex picture is to look at how the sea behaves. The primary or major force is very big waves or swell provided by the ocean. Extreme weather systems and planetary forces make this the dominant factor in the way the water moves. The secondary trend will be smaller waves that may occur from more localised weather conditions or reverberations from nearby land and obstacles. Unlike the big rolling waves in the primary trend, these smaller waves are shorter and sharper. They can run with or against the bigger waves they are between. The smallest waves, or ripples, will have the lowest impact and will come and go more quickly. A small boat in such a sea will feel all of these cycles to differing extents and so it is in financial markets. Charles Dow suggested three trends of differing periods but there may be several operating at once. Elliot Wave Theory is a form of technical analysis that seeks to resolve the differing waves and cycles. The most basic component of the theory is that prices move first in five waves and then reverse with three corrective waves retracing part of the initial five waves. The interpretation is fairly complex with a series of rules and is beyond the scope of this book.

Understanding the idea of higher highs and higher lows in an uptrend can help you hold your position when the market is panicking. In December 2009 oil was widely tipped in the media to have peaked and was due to fall back to price levels seen a year earlier. Around the middle of the month there were a few days of heavy selling in line with this prediction. While anything is possible, we should have known not to expect new lows below the September low of $65 as we had not first had a significant lower high. For a lower low to occur, we are likely to see a lower high first. It is the failure to go on and make new highs that is the important first sign that an uptrend might be failing. It is worth noting, we did have a lower high in July followed by a lower low, but this was really with a smaller trend within the more major trend. This does highlight the need for being able to break things down to the right trend which we will look at further in Chapter 10.

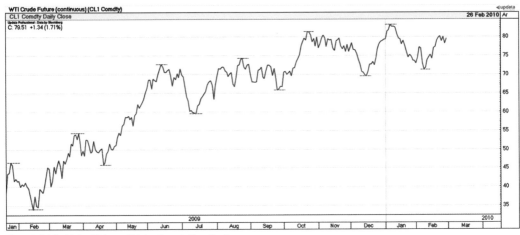

Chart 2-1: The higher highs and higher lows in the oil price

So the key characteristic of an uptrend is higher highs and higher lows. And for a downtrend it is lower lows and lower highs. This sounds fairly obvious, but, under pressure even the most experienced traders can overlook this.

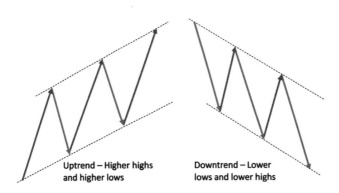

Uptrend – Higher highs and higher lows

Downtrend – Lower lows and lower highs

Figure 2-6: How to recognise uptrends and downtrends

## Trend lines - Support and Resistance

Even if you are new to Technical Analysis you may still have come across the terms 'resistance' and 'support' we have identified so far. As there has been a wider acceptance that price moves can be on purely technical grounds, commentators can be heard saying 'prices are finding support' or 'such and such is hitting resistance'. Levels of support and resistance are determined by previous highs and lows. As we have explained, these are the levels at which market participants have sold and bought respectively before.

Most price histories will have these key horizontal levels contained within them. Here we see a bar chart of the Norwegian Krone versus the US Dollar. Each bar represents a days trading range. Note the number of times the Krone hit resistance right at the 7.3060 level. This was a level the US Dollar could not break (i.e. the Dollar is worth more Krone). Horizontal levels show up particularly well in charts of currencies.

Chart 2-2: Norwegian Krone showing previous trading range

The more times a line of resistance or support is touched, the stronger it becomes. But all trends are broken in the end too. The ideal number of touches to define a line of support or resistance is three and it is rare to have more than six or seven exact touches. In fact it is quite often the case that by the time you can spot a good long trend clearly, it will soon break, which is why early identification of a trend change and a new counter trend forming is vital to making the trend your friend.

Support and resistance lines can also slope up or down, reflecting the change in prices over time. Here we see the UK stock market adhering to a very clear line of support in an uptrend over a four year period. Six precise touches of this nature is an unusually high number. Trends lines on stock market indices are not always this clear cut.

Chart 2-3: FTSE 100 Index with clear line of support

## Art or Science?

Technical Analysis is not an exact science. It can't be, given that some amount of price movement will be random and unpredictable. Many experienced technicians would argue that there is a knack to it and you definitely cannot be too precise, especially when it comes to defining levels of resistance and support. Below we see a weekly chart of the UK stock market over 13 years with key levels running through the price history (computer generated in fact). The low point of 2003 was almost exactly the level we found support again in 2009 on this chart. But in 2007, the high that the market reached was not quite as high as the high point set in early 2000. Did we hit an area of resistance in 2007 or not? The tops did occur in similar places and it would be hard to argue that market participants didn't sell at similar levels as several years earlier.

The lines running through the middle of this chart are key lines of action and are also approximate levels where prices found resistance or support. We often see resistance and support become interchangeable. Sellers at a previous resistance level are now buyers at the new level of support and vice versa. Once a key price level is breached it will often undergo a 'confirmation' by testing that same price level from the other side. On this chart you could argue that the 5,500 area has been pivotal in the past which may play on prices again at these levels.

Chart 2-4: FTSE 100 Index with key price levels

## Continuation or Reversal?

While the more touches you have of a line of support or resistance confirms that level to be stronger, the simple idea of breaking the previous significant high or low should always dominate your thinking on the chart. Frequently you will be faced with either of the two scenarios shown on the next page which are effectively a mirror of each other.

In the first case prices going higher than H would be a bullish (bulls are buyers) sign. Remember new highs are good from a technical perspective, with people now prepared to pay more than they were before. If prices fell back below L, we would have made a lower high than H, with the subsequent lower low. That would be bearish (bears are sellers). In the second example the reverse would apply. A break below L would be a new low – bearish, we are going lower still. A break above H, a new high – bullish, a reversal is taking place.

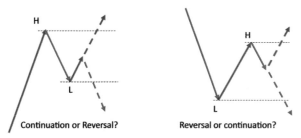

Figure 2.7: Understanding when we have a continuation of a reversal

When prices pull back or pause for breath like this, it is generally called a consolidation phase. Because prices spend more time trending than they do reversing, it is more likely that these phases are just a small part of a bigger trend. As a general rule, the direction prices leave a consolidation phase will be in the same direction they entered it. Hence this is also often called continuation. But, by definition, reversals in trend have to occur at some point too. We don't truly know whether a breakout in the direction of the trend has occurred until we pass the previous high or low. So it is nearly always best to wait for the break as confirmation. As a rough guide, consolidations should occur at least twice as often as reversals, but there are no hard and fast rules. Just know that prices are bullish above H and bearish below L and remind yourself of that whenever you first look at a chart.

## Patterns

There are a number of price patterns that technicians look for in charts to establish the likely direction of a price move and the potential extent of the move. This is one part of technical analysis that is more art than science. The patterns given here are the main ones with rules of thumb to follow. We will also come to see in subsequent chapters that Japanese technicians have their own set patterns which they use in conjunction with Cloud Charts. If you have a true understanding of support and resistance and the importance of higher highs and lower lows, then most patterns become clear on these criteria alone, saving you having to memorise all of them. Generally, patterns should almost leap out of the chart at you. If you cannot see a pattern easily, it is quite likely there isn't one there.

## Reversal patterns

As you might expect, top and bottom patterns are reversal patterns. There are several variations, but double tops and double bottoms are the most common. Triple tops and bottoms also shown are less common, but more reliable as a reversal due to the extra testing of support and resistance. They will rarely be as precise as shown here. It is the identifiable 'pattern' of price behaviour that counts. Another rule of thumb is that the height of the pattern determines a similar measured move out of the pattern. The key thing again is to wait for the break to be sure the pattern is confirmed.

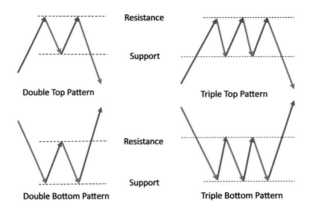

Figure 2-8: Tops and Bottoms

One of the most famous reversal patterns is the head and shoulders, where the price makes a lower high to form a second shoulder. It is probably the failure to make a new high that is more significant than the pattern itself. Once more the height of the pattern, the distance between the head and the neckline, determines the likely move once the break has occurred. The second should really occur on low volume and sometimes the neckline is confirmed from the other side once the break has occurred. Head and shoulders patterns can be sloping. Be careful, this pattern is not as common as most people think.
The pattern can also be inverted such that the measured move is upwards.

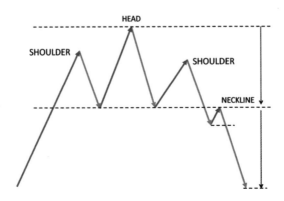

Figure 2-9: The Head and Shoulders Pattern (can aslo be inverted)

## Head and Shoulders Pattern

Chart 2-5: Chart shows a Head and Shoulders pattern

## Continuation patterns

These patterns generally follow the idea that the price exits the pattern in the direction that it entered, but there are exceptions and these patterns can fail. The other rule of thumb is that the extent of the move out of the pattern will be roughly equivalent to the extent of the move into the pattern. They are a rough guide to help you know what to expect if you spot them in a price chart. They are mostly variations on a theme of resistance and support lines converging toward each other. It is best to try and understand the psychology of the market participants with each pattern. The fact that prices are consolidating or squeezing after a run is indicative of the market uncertainty about where the price will go next. Remember it is normally best to wait for prices to break, but having a head start in knowing what is likely to happen from the pattern, can help you pounce on the breakout when it does occur.

Flags and Pennant patterns, shown below, are broadly similar to each other and are identified as their shape suggests. Pennants are a little more helpful with support and resistance converging on each other meaning they can't last forever. Whereas with Flags, you don't really know how long the sideways move will go on for.

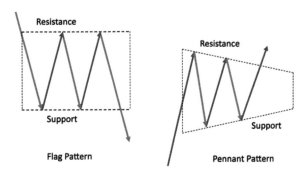

Figure 2-10: Flags and Pennants - normally continuation patterns

## Triangles

Triangle patterns in price movement are formed where the resistance and support lines converge on each other more sharply. The rules are that the break shall be in the direction (of the dissector) of the triangle, and that this normally will occur two thirds of the way along the triangle. Wedges are the exception, in terms of the direction of the breakout, in that the trend is so steep that it isn't normally feasible to breakout with even greater steepness. Hence the subsequent move in price goes against the direction in which the wedge points. Wedges are rarer than other triangle patterns and are in fact reversal patterns. Downward pointing wedges work in reverse.

The ascending triangle is where prices have rising support at the base with horizontal resistance at the top. Buyers are paying progressively more against sellers not letting prices go higher. The pattern is likely to be seen as a pause in the middle of an uptrend where some short term sideways resistance has emerged. The descending triangle works in reverse and is normally a continuation pattern during a downtrend. Symmetrical triangles tend to give quite powerful breakouts in either direction due to the sideways nature of the squeeze. The primary trend is your friend here, so the break should be in the direction the price entered the squeeze. Asymmetrical triangles are not that helpful as the price action is opening out giving fewer clues for when it will occur and it is likely to be weak without the squeeze effect of converging trend lines.

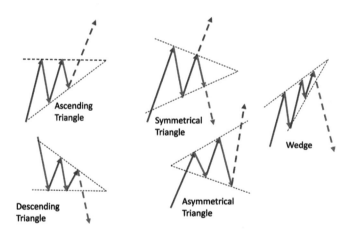

Figure 2-11: Triangle patterns

The chart below shows a descending triangle in German electricity prices. This was a reversal instead of a continuation pattern. The lower highs are highlighted and when the rough support level was breached, prices moved down more quickly.

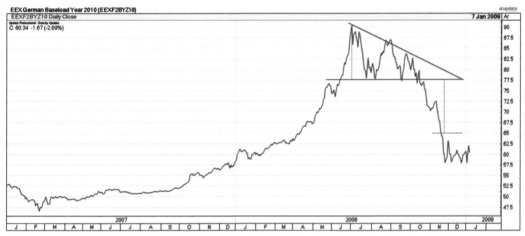

Chart 2-6: German Baseload electricity, descending triangle

The chart below shows a symmetrical triangle in gold prices which was a continuation pattern in this case.

Chart 2-7: Gold with symmetrical triangleTrend lines - Support and Resistance

The chart of the Euro below shows a sideways consolidation range which may be considered a flag.

Chart 2-8: Eurodollar with potential flag pattern

## Price behaviour in trends and mean reversion

We have already established that prices move in trends. We can see this more clearly by sampling data over a period using a statistical technique known as Least Squares Regression (LSR). The chart below shows how the stock price of IBM has moved over the last year or so. The LSR line is drawn through the data with parallel lines drawn two standard deviations from the LSR line. Statistically, two standard deviations will contain roughly 95% of prices and we see how when the outer bands are met, prices normally revert to the mean central trend.

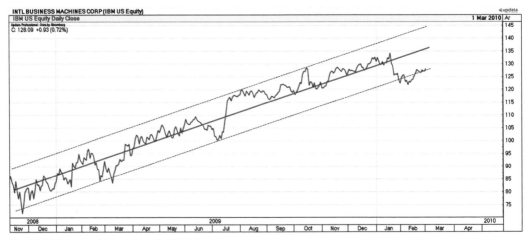

Chart 2-9: IBM chart with regression trend channel

In this case prices have tended to spend more time in the upper band of the trend channel as we might expect in an uptrend. Prices can move very quickly from one extreme to the other. In up-trends prices will frequently wander to the base of the trend before jumping sharply to the top of the trend channel. The reverse applies in downtrends where sharp moves down to the base of the trend are more likely. This staircase movement in price is a key characteristic of price behaviour in trends. The patterns we have identified in this chapter will often occur within a trend channel in the price. In the example above we also see prices wandering out of the up-trend channel. The failure to reach the top of the channel and prices not rebounding at the base support line has led to a deterioration of prices and the likely end of the uptrend. Volatility at the end of a trend, where prices move beyond the two standard deviations is normally a sign that a price trend is ending.

## Volume

Charles Dow was the first to highlight the importance of volume over a century ago. Trends ideally need to be confirmed by higher than normal volume to be taken more seriously. But volume data can be problematic. For instance with currencies, volume isn't reported with each trade. With stocks some trades might be broker to broker and it isn't clear where buying or selling went on. Some trades are reported as much as a few days later in some markets. And with the emergence of competing exchanges and platforms (sometimes knows as dark pools) and more and more derivatives such as Contracts for Difference, it is difficult to get an overall picture in volume. With commodities, trading volume can occur across a different series of contracts. In this area there is lots of Over the Counter trading or Off Exchange dealing between brokers and this data may not be available either. Most of all many different instruments are not sufficiently heavily traded such that spotting trends in volume can be difficult. Liquidity of trading is a major issue in areas such as small capitalisation stocks and trading in some commodities. It is well known among technicians that the more heavily something is traded, the better technical analysis will work. Lack of liquidity means prices are more at the mercy of large trades of the big market players in a given instrument. Volume charts are normally displayed in a histogram format with each day's volume represented as a vertical bar as shown below. The volume bars can be colour coded, as they are in this chart, according to whether we had an up day or a down day.

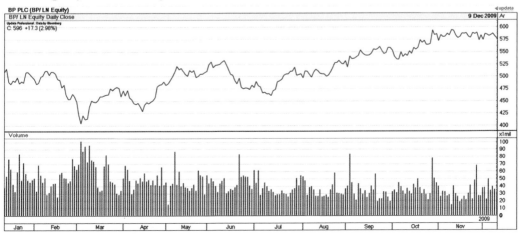

Chart 2-10: BP shares with daily volume bars in lower window

One of the problems of this histogram representation is that it is quite difficult to get an overall picture of volume. This can be addressed by using a cumulative volume measure such as On Balance Volume (OBV), devised by Joe Granville in the 1960s. This moving line is calculated over the price history by adding volume to the cumulative total on days where the price has closed higher than the previous day's close and subtracting the volume on a down day. We can see in the chart below how the cumulative line is much easier to read than the individual bars. Trend lines can also be applied to these charts in a similar manner as with price charts.

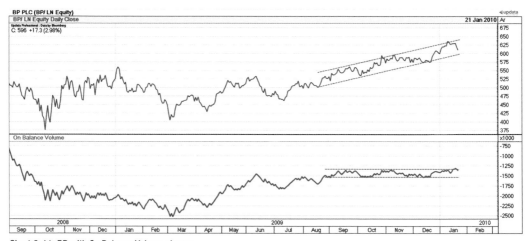

Chart 2-11: BP with On Balance Volume shown

## Divergence

The idea of convergence and divergence between two different charts is a common theme in technical analysis. Charles Dow highlighted this when he proposed that the Industrials and the Transports Averages need to confirm one another for a buy or sell signal to be trusted. His assessment that trends needed high volume to be believed was also in line with the idea of what we now call convergence and divergence and OBV is especially good for spotting this.

If we look at the same chart above, we see BP shares breaking to new highs, but the OBV chart isn't doing the same (i.e. not converging). In fact, here, the cumulative volume in BP started breaking down in October and went sideways while the BP share price continued going up for a few more weeks before going sideways as well. When BP broke to new highs the OBV didn't, which is divergence. Is the breakout valid? Well, the price has broken out which is bullish, but you would be wary of the breakout until the OBV moves higher. If OBV breaks to new lows in this BP example, that would be a bearish sign.

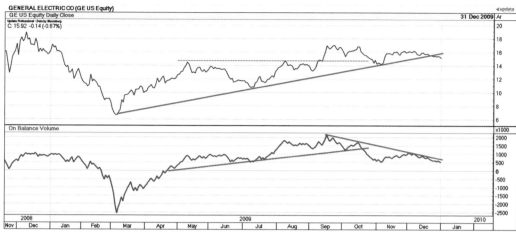

Chart 2-12: GE showing divergence with On Balance Volume

The chart above of GE shows how the OBV uptrend turned and broke to new lows while the GE share price continued to rise. How can this be happening? Whenever you see divergence (and it needs to be pretty clear) it is worth reminding yourself how the line or indicator is calculated. In the case of OBV, we know that volume is added to the line on up days and subtracted on down days. So if the price is still going up while OBV is falling it means that on up days there is not much volume and on down days there is a lot more. This clever distribution of shares is a great clue that there are early sellers in the market. Of course the same applies in reverse and here we see an example of accumulation of Volkswagen shares before prices started to rise.

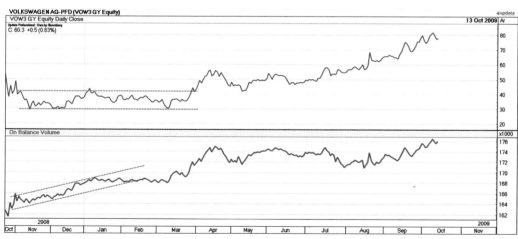

Chart 2-13: Volkswagen with divergence between price and On Balance Volume

Divergence is an idea that is vital in reading other technical analysis indicators as we will see in later chapters.

## Summary points

- The trend is your friend. Don't trade against it
- You can only truly know a top or a bottom retrospectively
- Higher highs and higher lows are what we expect in an uptrend
- Lower highs and lower lows are what we expect in a downtrend
- It is likely that three or more trends are acting on prices at a given time
- Always try to identify the key levels, or areas, of support and resistance for prices
- Continuation patterns occur more frequently in line with the trend than reversals
- The move in prices out of a pattern is often similar in magnitude to the move into the pattern
- Prices will revert to the mean during the trend
- Volatility in prices after a long period of trending is normally a sign of a trend reversal
- Volume is best represented as a cumulative line, look for divergence with the price chart

# Chapter 3 - **Moving Averages**

With On Balance Volume we looked at a moving cumulative line that was building each day with a simple arithmetic calculation. Moving averages are also a rolling calculation but the value of the average on each day is arrived at by looking back over a period. So for a simple 10 day average we start at the beginning of the price history and on day 10 we add all the prices together for the last 10 days and divide by 10 to get the average price. This value is the first plot of our moving average. On the next day we look back 10 days such that the first day is now not included in the calculation and plot the average again. So with each new day we take into the calculation, we drop the day 11 days ago out of the equation. And we move right through the history, such that the average of prices is changing, or 'moving', all the time.

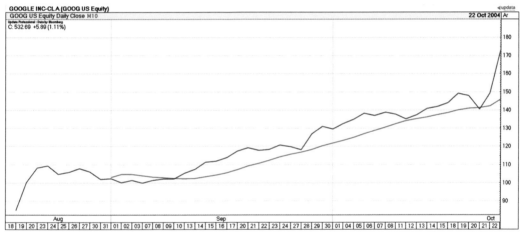

Chart 3-1: Google stock price chart with a simple 10 day moving average

Moving averages are normally drawn on the price chart because it is useful to understand where the price is in relation the average. If the price is above the average then prices are continuing to rise but if the price falls below the moving average this tells us that prices short term are falling faster than they have been throughout the averaging period. Think about the calculation again. For the price to suddenly fall through the average the most recent prices are so dramatically lower than those at the start of the period. As the oldest prices drop out of the calculation and the much lower new ones enter, that the price is now lower than its average. The average will take some time to catch up by replacing old high prices with new low ones each day.

## Signals

Understanding the way that the price and the average 'snake' about one another, due to the calculation, is synonymous to how Cloud Charts are constructed. So getting to grips with this section will stand you in good stead for mastering Cloud Chart analysis.

The most basic form of signal with moving averages is the price crossing the average. If the price falls through the average, that is a bearish signal, while a rise up through the average is bullish. In each case prices are moving so fast in a new direction as to be trend changing. The price crossing the average can be a good tool for helping you to spot a high or low retrospectively.

Before we look at other moving average signals it is worth noting that there are several ways to calculate a moving average beyond the simple linear calculation we have covered already. Many traders find simple averages are too slow to react to the latest price moves so they use an exponential average which assigns greater weight to the more recent prices in the calculation. The weighting factor will be between 0 and 1 and will decrease exponentially with each older price in the calculation. The most recent prices are given exponentially more weight, meaning the exponential moving average line will pull more towards faster moving price changes than the simple average.

Other moving averages include the weighted average, which applies more weight to the most recent prices but reduces on a linear basis. Adaptive averages adapt to market conditions by using a volatility ratio in their calculation. The regression average is quite different in that it is plotting the end point of the least squares regression line each day for the selected period. Proprietary averages such as the Indexia Average, are used by more sophisticated traders aiming to get keener results. These aim to strike an ideal medium with a combination of weighing and adaptive filtering.

Below we see a chart with six different average types on. We see the regression average gave a good sell signal at the top earlier and at a higher price level than the other averages. However, the price wandered through this same average too soon with a failed buy signal at the end of 2008. Each of these averages have their pros and cons but on balance the Indexia average has worked best here with earlier signals that have not transpired to be 'failed' signals.

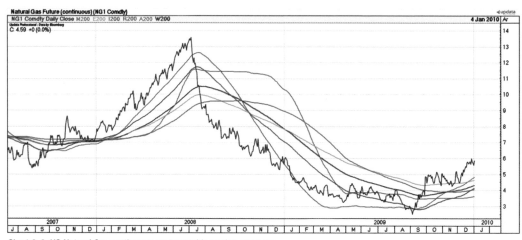

Chart 3-2: US Natural Gas continuous contract with moving averages

## Moving Average crossovers

One of the problems with using a single moving average and the price line is that the price can cut momentarily through the average. This whipsaw effect may lead you to act on what turns out to be a temporary blip. This can be addressed by using two moving averages of different periods to get more reliable cross over points between the averages themselves. The chart below shows the crossover of two commonly used moving averages, the 50 day and the 200 day. The first thing to notice is that there are fewer signals between the two averages than there would be with the price. When the shorter term average crosses above the longer term one, this is a 'golden cross' which is a bullish signal, while the shorter term average falling through the long term average is a 'dead cross', a bearish signal. It is worth noting here that the crossover signals between the two averages, while giving fewer false signals, do occur later as shown. This risk-reward conundrum of earlier riskier signals versus later less risky ones is another common theme in technical analysis as we will come to see.

Chart 3-3: Google stock with 2 moving averages

Some technicians consider that even two averages can give too many failed crossovers so they use a combination of three averages that must all cross each other for a signal. Here we see how the false signal with two averages was eliminated, but the signals are now even later still.

Chart 3-4: Google stock with 3 moving average

## Which periods to use

One of the biggest issues in using technical indicators is knowing which look-back period to use for the calculation of the indicator. There are a number of approaches but in each case consideration needs to be given to analysing the primary, secondary and shorter term trends in a price history. Technical traders often use averaging periods for their indicators without much consideration of the period itself.

It is important to remember that the number of trading days and calendar days in a given period are different and some people get confused by this. In nearly all countries there are five trading days in a week, ten in two weeks and 20 to 23 days in a month. This means a quarter is around 65 days and a year is usually 257 trading days.

The most commonly used periods are 10,20,50,100 and 200 days. Other periods frequently used are 14, 30, 60 and 90 days, perhaps in the belief they are two week, one month, two month and three month averages.

## Fibonacci numbers

The twelfth century Italian mathematician, Leonardo Pisano Bogollo, known as Leonardo of Pisa, or more commonly, Fibonacci is considered by many to be the biggest talent in mathematics of the middle ages. He was responsible for popularising the use of Hindu-Arabic numerals in Europe, recognizing that they were simpler and more efficient than roman numerals.

Fibonacci uncovered a series of mathematical relationships in the natural world. He showed that the growth in a hypothetical population of rabbits would be in line with his now famous Fibonacci sequence. This number series is produced by simply adding the two previous numbers in the series as below:

0, 1, 1, 2, 3, 5, 8, 13, 21, 34, 55, 89, 144, 233…..

Because technical analysis theory is rooted in the phenomenon of crowd behaviour, itself a natural phenomenon, many technicians rely on these numbers heavily for period selection in their technical indicators. The sequence also has some value as it is non linear, opening out with longer time frames. It is interesting to note that 13 is close to 14 often used by technicians, 21 is approximately the number of trading days in a month and 233 is close to the number of trading days in a year. If you don't want to put some work into period selection 8, 13, 21 and 34 (and combinations of these) are generally good numbers to use.

## Estimating the cycle period

Another method for choosing a look-back period for indicators is to attempt to estimate the cycle period. The reasoning is that it is best to try to sample as near as possible the data across the full cycle when calculating a rolling line such as an average. If you select a number where you are only sampling say 3/5 of the full cycle you are affectively missing data in your line calculation. It is best to try and match the cycle if you can, especially if the periodicity is clear. Estimating the cycles in a price history is often a useful exercise in itself to gain an understanding of the trends within trends and when a cycle high or cycle low might be due to occur. If you know you are near the high point or low point of a cycle on a given day you may trade accordingly.

You can measure cycles quite simply by looking at the distance between successive peaks or troughs of the line through the middle of the cycle as shown below.

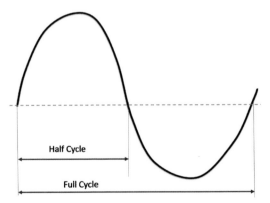

Figure 3-1: It is best to sample the data for a half or a full cycle

But of course price histories rarely follow such a clear cut cycle and you will be left to use some artistic licence to arrive at the approximate cycle periods.

Here we see some examples of estimating the period. In the first chart we have used a simple tool to line up the low points in the price history.

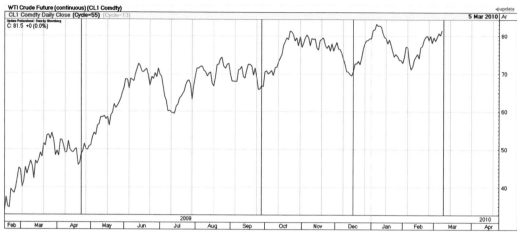

Chart 3-5: Oil with cycle periods measured from low points

In certain cases, measuring the cycle lows (or highs) might be hard to do visually. One possibility is to use a least squares regression trend across the section of pricehistory you are analysing. The cycle can then be measured from where the price cuts down through the central trend to the next point where it does it again. The chart below shows this.

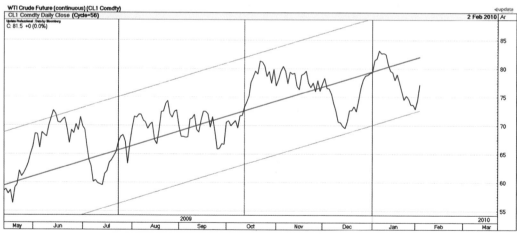

Chart 3-6: Oil with cycle periods measured with crosses of central regression trend

Another quick and simple way to arrive at periods that work well for an indicator is to use some trial and error with different periods, such that unwanted signals disappear. This is normally pretty quick and easy to do with most technical analysis software programs.

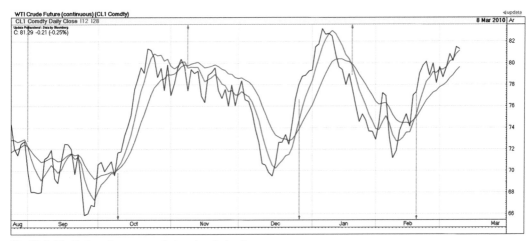

Chart 3-7: Oil with 2 moving averages that work well visually

## Back-testing for the best periods (optimising)

As computers and software have become more powerful, it is possible to arrive at the periods that produced the best (normally defined as profit) results historically in a matter of seconds. We will look at back-testing in more detail in Chapter 10, but there are two ways to test. The first is to test the periods you are using to see how well they worked. The second is to specify a range of periods to test. Here we see the results from optimising two moving averages on the chart below. You may choose to use these exact average periods for signals but it is worth noting that the periods that have been optimum in the past won't necessarily be optimum in the future. Re-running the optimisations fairly frequently is one way to deal with this. A back-test is probably more useful in telling you if the periods you are using are close to optimum. One method is to run the back-tests and then select the Fibonacci numbers that are nearest the results.

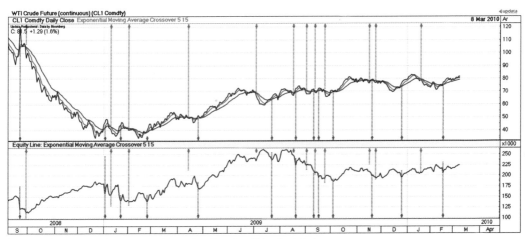

Chart 3-8: Oil with 2 moving averages that produced most profit in a back-test

## Moving Averages for trend definition

Perhaps one of the most useful functions a moving average can serve is in helping to define the prevailing trend. As a trend following tool, averages are usually considered to give signals which are too late to be useful for most traders. The average does however help you know whether the price is running higher above average and is hence bullish. If prices are falling more quickly, below the average and faster, this is bearish. Longer term averages can also be used as a simple trend filter to help you eliminate counter trend signals. For instance, in the chart below, we could take all the golden cross buy signals above the longer term 65 day average for buy signals and the dead crosses below the long term averages for sell signal. A different tool for a keener exit could be used. This is one way of ensuring the longer term trend is your friend.

Chart 3-9: Eurodollar with long term average as a trend filter for shorter term crossovers

## Moving Averages on indicators

Moving averages can also be useful on other indicators as a signal line. A 90 day average on the OBV chart for Whitbread shows how the volume trend has changed. This can give a better view of when an indicator has changed direction.

Chart 3-10: On Balance Volume with a moving average highlighting volume trend

## Moving Average Bands

In the previous chapter we looked at defining a trend channel by setting two parallel lines either side of a central straight regression line. This can also be done using a moving average as the central line, creating a trading envelope by shifting copies of the average higher and lower. This forms a channel or zone of commitment and helps in gauging overbought and oversold conditions. Moves in price outside the bands are the extreme conditions, overbought (above the top band) or oversold (below the bottom band). The distance at which the bands are set is a percentage of the price. So now we have two variables, the average period and the percentage where the bands are set. This could also be optimised for both variables. Here we see moving average bands for Cairn Energy with a 21 day averaging period with 5 percent bands.

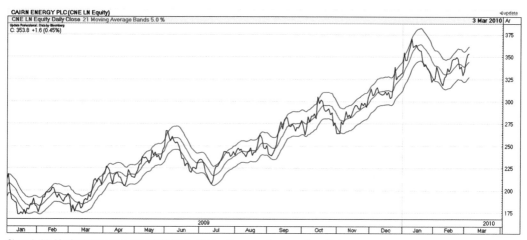

Chart 3-11: Moving average bands highlighting when prices are a long way from their average

## Bollinger Bands

Bollinger Bands, an idea developed by John Bollinger, are similar to moving average bands, except that the width of the bands is determined by volatility. The bands are plotted a defined number of standard deviations from the average. This means the bands are self adjusting, in that they widen in volatile markets and narrow during calmer periods.

John Bollinger swears by the 20 period average with the bands plotted at 2 standard deviations from the price and advocates one of the most valuable aspects of the bands is when a 'squeeze' occurs. This is when the volatility is historically low and the bands have pulled very close together. As with the price patterns described earlier, this convergence of the bands is a precursor to a breakout. The chart below shows the break from a squeeze in the Bollinger bands.

Chart 3-12: Bollinger Bands 'squeezing' together on low volatility

## Summary points

- Price crossing a moving average is an earlier riskier signal
- Two or three moving averages crossing on another give more reliable signals
- Common periods are 14, 20, 50, 60, 90 and 200
- Fibonacci numbers – 13, 21, 34 often work well
- Identifying the cycle period is helpful to ensure your averaging period is close
- Optimising averaging periods in back-tests is a way to establish which periods work best
- Moving averages are useful for trend definition on the price chart
- Moving averages can be used on indicators, such as On Balance Volume, to generate signals
- Moving average bands and Bollinger Bands can be used to identify if prices are overbought or oversold
- Bollinger Band squeezes can help identify and impending dramatic move in prices

# Chapter 4 - **Indicators**

In technical analysis, there is a whole group of indicators, sometimes known as oscillators, which are typically displayed in a bottom window below the price chart. Like moving averages they are based on a rolling calculation and normally require a look-back period. The points on choosing periods for moving averages covered in the previous chapter generally apply to periodic indicators as well.

Many indicators are first derivative measures of the price. It is useful to use the analogy of distance, speed and acceleration to get a feel for what most indicators are trying to measure. Speed is distance over time (first order) and acceleration (second order) is speed over time. If you imagine pulling away from a stationary position at a set of traffic lights in a car, to begin with you are not moving very fast, but the rate at which your speed is changing is dramatic. You feel the back of the seat against you from the force of accelerating. Once you have reached the speed limit, you are going fast but your speed is near constant such that you have no acceleration. As you approach the next set of traffic lights you apply the brakes, feeling yourself being pushed forward as you slow down. Your speed is in fact changing fastest when you feel these forces of acceleration and deceleration, but it is not clearly apparent by looking out the window as you might be going very slowly or very fast respectively. Second order oscillators are trying to show up these changes in acceleration in order to get a heads up on how the speed of prices will change. Is the price about to take off or is it coming to a halt?

An indicator that demonstrates prices changing speed is Momentum, which measures the rate of change in price over a chosen period. This line, normally shown below the price, oscillates above or below a zero line showing times of positive and negative velocity respectively. Rising momentum above zero indicates prices are rising with increasing speed. Falling momentum above zero indicates prices are still rising but the speed of the rise is slowing. If we are below zero and falling, prices are falling at a gathering pace, while rising below zero means prices are still falling but the speed of the full is slowing.

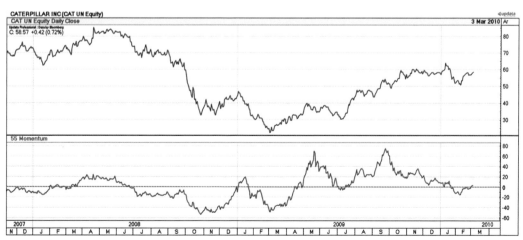

Chart 4-1: Caterpillar with 55 day momentum

Another simple indicator is the overbought/oversold indicator (OBOS) which is simply the percentage distance between a moving average and the price. So when the price cuts up through the moving average the OBOS line crosses the zero level at the same time. The real advantage we gain with this indicator is that we see the extreme points where the price is at its furthest from the average and as this turns we have some idea that prices are returning to the average rate of change. Another valuable aspect is that we can put the current position of such an oscillator into an historical context by looking back over the history. In the chart below, it would be hard to say from the top window alone when the price had moved a long way from its moving average, but the OBOS line makes this clear immediately, because it is a measure of this distance.

Chart 4-2: HP with overbought/oversold (OBOS) indicator

## MACD

The Moving Average Convergence Divergence (MACD) devised by Gerald Appel, often called the 'Mac D', takes this idea a stage further by measuring the distance between two moving averages. So this requires both averaging periods to be specified.

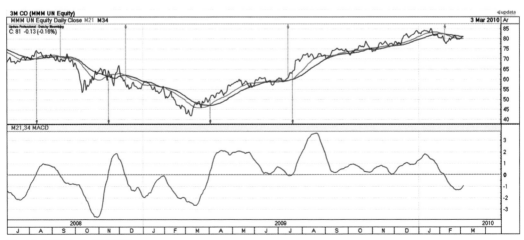

Chart 4-3: 3M stock with MACD

A variation on the MACD line is the MACD histogram, which is a derivative of the MACD calculation. We identified that we can use a moving average on an oscillator as a signal line. In the same way that we use MACD to understand the distance between averages, the histogram shows us the distance between the MACD and an average of that MACD, the signal line. The preferred settings for this are to use exponential averages 12 and 26 days, with a 9 day exponential average calculated on the MACD line itself. This means instead of the price being used for the 9 day signal line, the MACD values are being used. The distance between the MACD and the Signal line is displayed as a histogram and the value of this is that you can spot the move away from an extreme the day it happens with a bar that is lower than the extreme. It may turn out not to be the extreme, but it often is the first sign of the MACD slowing down. The shorter term average is pulling back towards the longer term one. Prices are decelerating.

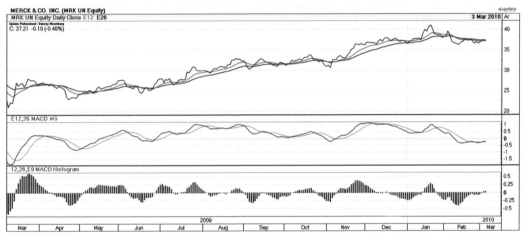

Chart 4-4: Merck with MACD and MACD Histogram

## Welles Wider RSI

J. Welles Wilder invented a number of oscillators in the 1970's but he is most famous for his Relative Strength Index. The RSI is not related to Relative Strength (covered on page 65) and therefore it is good idea to just call it 'RSI' and not get confused.

The indicator is a smoothed, weighted velocity index with a fixed scale ranging between 0 and 100, which has the advantage that the RSI reading can be quickly understood. It is customary that a reading below 30 is considered to be in the oversold zone and a reading over 70 is overbought. A buy signal is given when the RSI moves up through 30 and a sell signal is given when the RSI moves down through 70. A period of 14 is commonly used.

It is worth pointing out that quite a number of technical analysis systems (including some leading market terminals) and web sites calculate the RSI incorrectly. Wilder's formula uses a non-standard averaging technique, so make sure that the RSI you are using is correct in this regard.

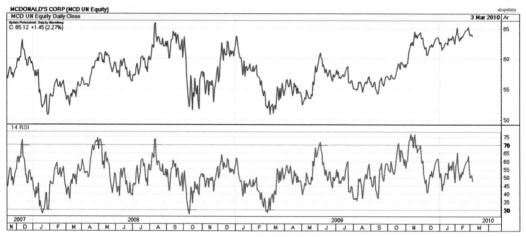

Chart 4-5: McDonald's stock with 14 day RSI

Wilder also invented the Directional Movement Chart, which is better known for its ADX line. The indicator comprises three lines, and attempts to measure trend quality and direction. The Positive Directional Indicator (+DI) measures the percentage of up movement over the look-back period specified and the Negative Directional Indicator (-DI) shows the down movement. When +DI crosses above –DI a buy signal is indicated, while a sell is when the +DI crosses below the –DI. The Average Directional Movement Index the trend on a scale of 0 to 100. The higher the ADX value, the stronger the prevailing uptrend or downtrend. A warning of a buy signal is given each time the ADX line direction changes and this normally occurs around the same time as the +DI and –DI cross. This chart also comprises an ADXR value which is the average value of the ADX line over the same look-back period specified for the Directional Movement lines. The ADXR value is commonly used to define whether an instrument is trending or not. If the ADXR is greater than 25 it is trending while a value below 20 means it is non trending. This will also vary for different instruments and the value will alter with the look-back period chosen. Getting the period right with indicators is half the battle. Here we see the Direction Movement chart for Hewlett Packard where in the first half of 2009 prices were non-trending with the ADX value predominantly below the 25 level. From July to December, prices were trending according to this measure.

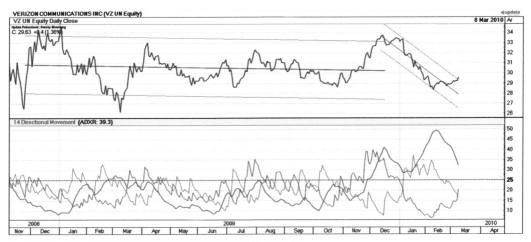

Chart 4-6: Verizon with Directional Movement, trending with ADX above 25

## How well has an indicator worked?

Indicators drawn in a bottom window like the ones we have just covered are useful for putting the indicator's current position into an historical context. Looking back over time, we can see where the peaks and troughs normally occur. It is important to relate indicator signals back to the price chart to see how well they have worked. It is always worth conducting this visual check. Here we see another indicator called the Coppock which is one of the oldest technical indicators for analysing stock markets. It adds together the 14 and 11 month percentage changes and then takes a 10 month weighted total of this to create the Coppock line. It is a monthly indicator and therefore is looking for a long-term change. It is renowned for long-term buy signals, and not really used for sell signals. The idea is that when the Coppock turns from a fall and starts rising, this is a buy signal. Here we can see the value of the historically low turning points over a century. Looking at what levels the Coppock line turned off lows and relating that to low points in the price chart, we can decide at what levels we would choose to ignore turning points in the indicator for signals.

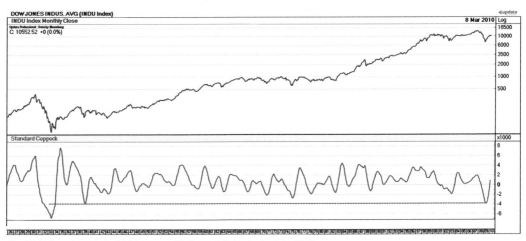

Chart 4-7: Dow Jones Industrial Average with Coppock Indicator back to 1920s

## Optimising indicator periods

In the previous chapter we saw that moving averages could be optimised in back-tests to arrive at the periods that produced the most profit over a period. This can be done with indicators as well and here we see such a test on Google using the Commodity Channel Index. This breakout indicator, devised by Donald Lambert, is meant to give a buy signal when the line rises through -100 and a sell when it falls through +100. Running computer optimisation using these criteria testing each period between 14 and 55 days shows that 37 days produced the best profit line, known as an equity curve, when entering a long position with a rise through -100 and exiting when the line falls through +100. Such optimisations can be run on any indicator to establish the best periods to use as well as the best levels signals are given at.

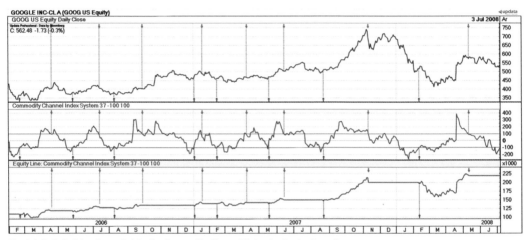

Chart 4-8: Optimising the period for the Commodity Channel Index for the best results

## Indicators of indicators

Indicators can in fact be drawn on themselves. We saw with MACD how a moving average of the MACD could be used to create the MACD Histogram. It is equally valid to produce a second order derivative such as Momentum of Momentum. Here we see a 5 day Momentum of the 21 day Momentum on the Dow Jones Index to highlight the speed at which the market was turning in March 2009.

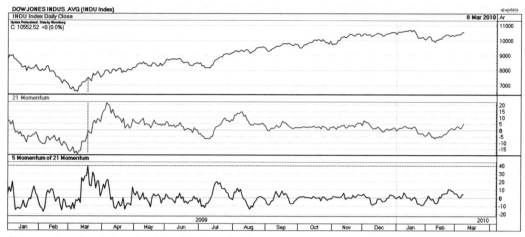

Chart 4-9: Momentum of Momentum for the Dow Jones IA Index

## Proprietary and custom programmed indicators

The indicators we have covered so far are just a handful of the mainstream ones that
are used and that you will readily find in most software systems or on web sites. There
are many others such as Stochastic (Regular and Slow), Directional Oscillator, Chaikin
Volatility, Money Flow, Average True Range, Williams Accumulation/Distribution,
Williams %R, to name just a few. Many systems include pre-programmed proprietary
indicators, and there are really no limits with built in programming languages. Indicator
libraries can be found online with literally hundreds, if not thousands, of unique indicators
available. Furthermore, powerful computer software enables you to back-test how well
any given tool works. You just need to be able to define the entry and exit signals.

Below we see INDEXIA Market Tracker, which is an example of a proprietary indicator. This highlights how indicators can look very different. The indicator has its foundation in econometrics and attempts to assign probabilities to expected price movement. It ranges between -100 and +100 and is effectively saying that at -100 there is a 100% chance that the price will rise and a 100% probability of a fall at +100. These levels are rarely reached, but you can see from the indicator here that prices can remain near the extremes for quite some time. It is the moves out of the overbought and oversold zones that are the signal of a change. These levels can be decided upon visually as has been done in the chart below, or you can optimise with a back-test for the most profitable period to use. Both the look-back period for the indicator calculation, and the levels at which the signals are given can be optimised. The Market Tracker does deal with the problem that prices can be in an overbought or oversold state for some time. Other indicators could be giving signals in this sort of situation, whereas here it is the move from these regions which is the sign that prices are set to turn.

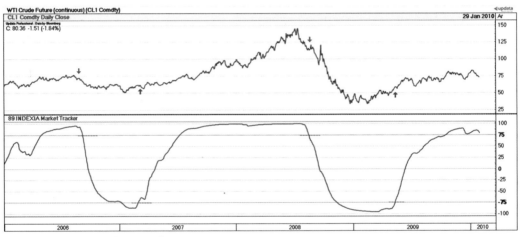

Chart 4-10: INDEXIA Market Tracker on Oil

## Divergence

As we discovered with On Balance Volume, the divergence between price and an indicator can give us an indication as to what the price is going to do next. You will see divergence frequently with indicators, but it does not always mean the price will follow suit. It is nearly always best to wait for the breakout in the price to occur. If prices become range bound or one of the price patterns we covered in Chapter 2 is forming, indicators might well give you a clue as to the direction of the break. The chart below shows how the OBOS, Momentum and RSI indicators were all 'basing' and trending upwards while the price was in a sideways range.

This suggested a break to the upside, and, as it happened that is what occurred soon after. It is a useful lesson that indicators can help you when markets are stuck in a sideways trading range.

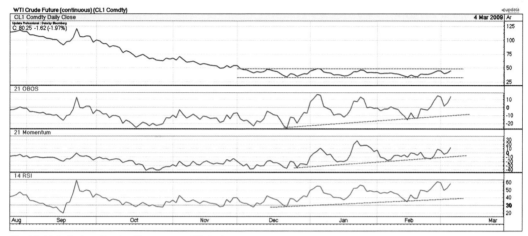

Chart 4-11: Indicators showing divergence on Oil chart

The most important thing to remember about indicators is that they are just that – indicators! They can only give you an indication of what prices should do and you should always wait for prices to break and confirm what the indicators suggest.

## Relative Strength

A very simple technical analysis technique is to divide one price chart by another price chart to asses relative performance. The resulting relative strength chart shows every daily point as the value of the first price history divided by the second. This is useful for isolating the effect of the denominator chart from the instrument you are trying to look at. This is particularly valuable in stock analysis where fund managers are focused on their performance relative to the market.

So, for the stock of Cisco Sytems below, we have a relative strength chart against the Dow Jones index. This chart shows the stock's true performance, with the market effects taken out. It is important to note that relative strength can be rising when the stock is in fact falling, i.e. the stock is not falling as fast as the market. It can also be falling when the stock is rising, if the market is falling more quickly. The relative strength chart here is 'normalised' to 100 on a chosen date so that we can easily read the percentage performance thereafter off the right hand axis.

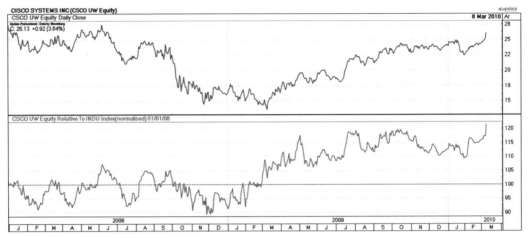

Chart 4-12: Cisco Systems relative to the Dow Jones IA Index

Fund Managers will often look at only relative strength charts of stocks by replacing the price history with a relative strength chart as their default. The same technical analysis techniques we have discussed can be carried out on the relative chart and interpreted in the same way. An example is shown below.

Chart 4-13: Walt Disney, Momentum of Relative Strength

While relative strength is normally used for stocks, it can also be used in any situation where you want to isolate an underlying influence in order to see the true performance of something. For instance if you believe that electricity prices are heavily driven by the price of oil, a relative chart will effectively remove the impact of such a price driver out of the relative strength chart.

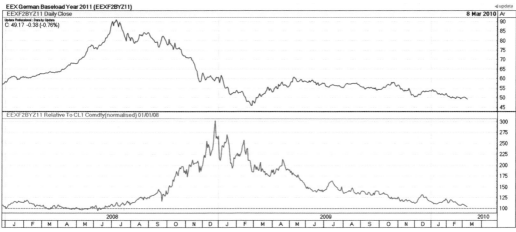

Chart 4-14: German Baseload Electricity (Cal 11) relative to Oi

## Spread Charts

Spreads are heavily used in commodity and energy trading. This is where one price chart is subtracted from another to get a difference between the two and to see how that difference varies. For instance, in a given commodity, you may wish to see the difference between a shortest dated contract (near) and the next dated contract (far), and how that difference varies. This is typically called a Calendar Spread. Spread charts can involve a number of instruments and other factors too. Energy traders use different spreads for pricing and trading electricity contracts. Spark spreads show the theoretical gross margin of power generated from gas by applying the cost of gas and a heat rate. Dark spreads work similarly with coal. These spreads can also take account of the emissions cost. The resulting spread chart can move if coal or gas moves or the price of traded carbon credits is changing. The key thing from a technician's point of view is that these charts can be analysed too. Moving averages, for example, help ascertain where the turning points are occurring in the spread. An RSI could be optimised to develop a trading strategy on the spread chart itself. There are no real limits to how indicators can be applied to trading.

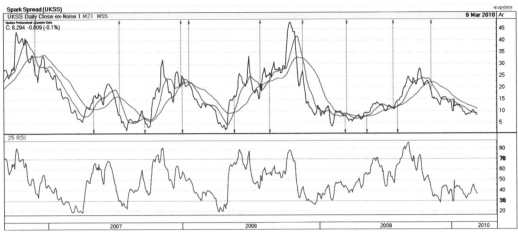

Chart 4-15: Moving averages and RSI on a Spark Spread

## Seasonality Charts

You can see by now that there are a lot of different ways to represent historical data with numerous technical analysis tools to interpret it. Seasonality charts work on the basis of looking at the same point in time in a week, a month or a year and plotting a predictive average of the prices going forward. This is especially good for commodities such as oil or gas, when the winter and summer seasons can have an effect, but they can easily be applied to stock markets too. For instance, the adage 'sell in May and go away, come back on St. Leger's Day (Oct)', has varied as a strategy for buying stocks as marked on the seasonal chart of the S&P 500 Index below. Again you can do analysis on the seasonal to see when signals might occur in future. The chart shows when 55 and 89 day moving averages cross on the seasonal chart in the future. The seasonal chart is not infallible as it is just shows the average price behaviour over previous years and projects that average into the future. Its main purpose is to highlight the season effect of how prices typically move.

Chart 4-16: Seasonality of the US stockmarket

## Correlation

Many traders consider correlation between different asset classes to be their lifeblood. Some trade correlated pairs of instruments and others look for non-correlated pairs. Hedge Funds constantly search for non-correlated assets for improved portfolio diversity and the ability to trade these non-correlated assets with Exchange Traded Funds (ETFs) has been greater than ever. Correlation looks at the relationship between price movement each day for two different instruments and assesses how related those moves are. For instance, for a correlation over the last 65 days between two instruments, the point of intersection of each price on each of the 65 days is plotted. An ordinary least squares regression line that best fits the data is drawn. The y axis intercept is the alpha value, the slope of the line is known as beta, but the most quoted correlation measure is the correlation coefficient expressed as a percentage. Here we see the 65 day correlation between German Baseload Electricity and oil.

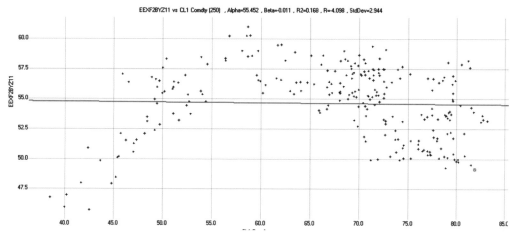

Chart 4-17: Correlation between German Baseload electricity price and Oil

Part of the problem with correlation relationships is that they are changing all the time. This makes them ripe for charting the historical change, to get an understanding of whether a correlation value is high or low in an historical context. Perhaps, more importantly, a historical chart of the correlation coefficient helps us understand whether the correlation is increasing or decreasing.

It is a commonly held view that when commodity prices rise the US dollar falls and vice verse. So with the Euro generally moving in the opposite direction to the US dollar, this should mean that the Euro and Oil prices are strongly correlated. The fact that Oil fell by almost 80% in 2008 and the Euro didn't, does make you start to question this idea. We see from the historical correlation charts below that, indeed, oil and the Euro are highly correlated, with a 250 day (a year) look-back, most of the time. But there was a period in early 2009 where they were negatively correlated – i.e. Oil goes up, the US dollar goes up too, which flies in the face of a widely held idea. We also see here that the shorter term 65 day correlation is changing from correlated to uncorrelated frequently.

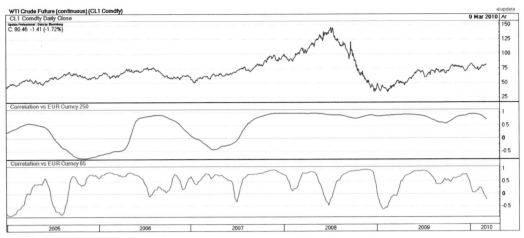

Chart 4-18: Historic correlation Oil and Euro

Another widely held relationship is that high commodity prices are bad news for stock markets. If the oil price goes up, the stock market will fall due to all the inflationary ramifications. But we see from the chart below that through much of 2009 the stock market and the oil price were highly correlated on the longer term measures. Commodity traders began to see the opening of world equity markets as sentiment indicator for trading in their own instruments. The problem is, that just as you have cottoned onto this idea, the relationship changes, so having a handle on how it is changing can be very helpful.

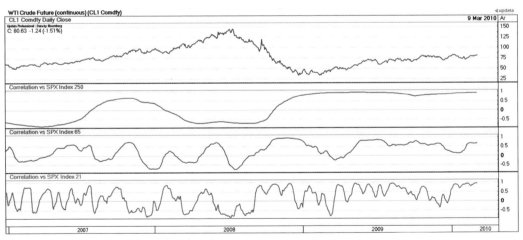

Chart 4-19: Historic correlation Oil and US stock market

The correlation charts confirm something that most experienced technical analysts have known for years. Widely held views in the market and what you might read in the press always need to be challenged or confirmed by looking at the charts. The charts don't lie about what is really happening. Always check them before taking an idea at face value.

## Log scale charts

It is sometimes desirable to chart price histories on a log scale where the y axis is non-linear to reflect the percentage change in prices. Some technicians only look at log scale charts and have these set as their default. There are two main reasons you would choose to look at a price history in log scale terms, and both are about removing curvature that appears as a result of a dramatic change. The first instance is for charts over a very long time period where price changes have been dramatic. Here we see a chart of the Dow Jones Index over the last 40 years. The top chart is on an arithmetic scale and the bottom one is on a log scale. Notice how the price behaviour early on in the chart, at price levels much lower than today, is clearer. The uptrend is clearer on the log scale chart as well.

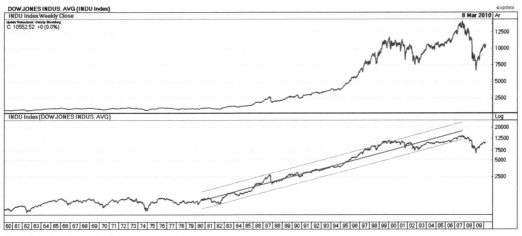

Chart 4-20: Log Scale chart of Dow Jones IA Index

The other time to use a log scale chart is when prices move very quickly in a short space of time. Here we see arithmetic and log scale charts of Yahoo! below. The log scale chart is much easier to read. The technical analysis tools we have covered will work equally well on log scale charts. For instance on Yahoo! we see how moving signals are given in the same place on each chart.

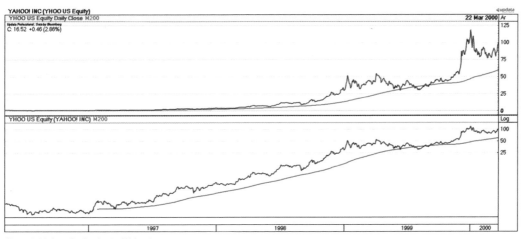

Chart 4-21: Log Scale chart of Yahoo!

## Flipping your charts

As we pointed out with the identification of patterns the inverted scenario invariably applies in reverse. So you can 'flip' your charts and view them upside down. Most of us have a bull or bear side bias. This is especially true if you are holding a position where the outcome of the chart is important. The chart below shows the recovery in the US stock market in 2009.

If you bought stocks a few years ago at higher levels than now you may well feel the market can recover further. If you sold a few years ago but missed the opportunity to get in soon after the 2009 lows, you may be saying to yourself 'prices can't go any higher'.

Chart 4-22: Chart of S&P 500 Index

Take the same chart and flip it up the other way and perhaps you can see more clearly that prices could easily fall further having made new lows. Of course what you are really saying, given the inverted picture, is prices could rise further having made new highs. Flipped charts will often also show up a top pattern (which is therefore a bottom) or a bottom pattern (which is therefore a top) more clearly. If you are uncertain about a chart, flipping can help you see things with renewed clarity by removing your inherent bias.

Chart 4-23: Chart of S&P 500 Index inverted or ' flipped'

# Fibonacci Retracements

We have already looked at the number sequence popularised by Fibonacci on page 50. The golden ratio said to be used by the Greeks over 1,000 years earlier is embedded in the sequence, although it is believed to have been fully proved three hundred years later by the renowned German astronomer Johannes Kepler. Looking at the number series again (produced by adding the two previous numbers) if we divide a number in the series by the previous number, from 55 onwards this settles to a constant value of 1.618.

0, 1, 1, 2, 3, 5, 8, 13, 21, 34, 55, 89, 144, 233.....

You can easily play with this yourself in a spreadsheet. The number is often denoted by the Greek letter phi ($\varphi$) and it has some quite unique mathematical properties. The reciprocal of 1.618 is 0.618 and $1 - 1.618 = -0.618$ for instance.

The golden ratio is apparent in dimensions in ancient Greek architecture. Artists for centuries have relied on this ratio for its visual properties. Leonardo da Vinci's famous Vitruvian man suggested the golden ratio was present in human proportions. The ratio of a person's total height to the height of their naval is typically around 1.618. Fibonacci numbers and the ratio have been shown to occur frequently in nature. Fibonacci attempted to model natural shapes such as the human ear or shells and constructed mathematical spirals from the golden ratio via a series of squares and rectangles.

Because of this presence of the ratio throughout nature, technicians have adopted it in an attempt to model crowd behaviour, itself a natural phenomenon. Apart from using the numbers for periods in time series data such as averages and indicators, the golden ratio may be used for measuring the extent of price moves. There are a number of books dedicated to Fibonacci analysis and Elliot Wave theory builds on this as well. These subjects are too broad to cover in this book and here we just show how the golden ratio can be used to project the levels which prices will retrace after a run from a low to a high and vice verse. Fibonacci Retracements highlight that not all technical analysis is time series analysis. It is also interesting to note that the main tenet of Elliot Wave Theory, is that prices move in a pattern of five waves in one direction, which is then partially retraced with three corrective waves, both Fibonacci numbers.

Chart 4-24: Fibonacci retracements for British Pound

A general rule of thumb with retracements is that most measured moves from a high or low will retrace themselves by around half that overall move. Key Fibonacci levels are marked on this chart but the most important ones are the 38.2% and the 61.8% levels. The 61.8% level comes from 0.618 and the 38.2% level comes from 1 - 0.618 = 0.382. Charles Dow noted that retracements of one third and two thirds were important. These retracement levels, among others, were also cited by W. D Gann a few decades later. Some may consider such retracements as, close enough to the key Fibonacci levels. Others will not, and expect them to be met precisely. Which highs and lows you choose to run your measure from to arrive at the right levels of retracement will govern your 'fib' levels. This makes this technique highly subjective for the newcomer to technical analysis. How the price interacts with the retracement levels early on can also provide credibility for the next levels. We see this in the example above. As you might expect, retracements can be applied the other way up where the price has fallen and you are looking to identify levels to which it will recover. Here is an example of for Johnson & Johnson below.

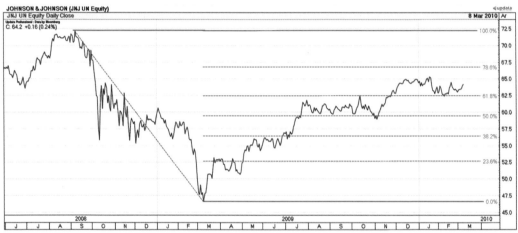

Chart 4-25: Fibonacci retracements for Johnson & Johnson

## Fibonacci Extensions

In Chapter 2, we looked at price patterns as an approximate way to arrive at future price targets. The Golden Ratio can also be used to project potential targets based on a retracement in price, known as Fibonacci Extensions. The same key percentage levels we used for retracements after a run in prices, are measured from the base of a corrective move as shown on the chart of the Euro.

Chart 4-26: Fibonacci extensions for Eurodollar

Fibonacci Extensions can be used in reverse and here we see how the initial fall in the Japanese stock market in 1990 projected key levels of price action in the years that followed.

Chart 4-27: Fibonacci extensions on Nikkei 225 Index

## Summary points

- Periodic indicators are generally used to identify price movement changing speed
- The methods for selecting indicator periods are the same as with moving averages
- Always relate indicator signals to the price chart to establish how well they have worked
- Unlimited proprietary indicators can be derived from virtually any formula and back-tested
- Look for Divergence between indicators and the price chart for a warning of price trends changing
- Divergence is useful in providing clues for the direction of breakouts for prices from a sideways trading range
- Relative Strength charts can isolate the effect of an underlying market to show and instruments true performance with the effect of that market
- Relative Strength charts can be analysed in the same way as price charts
- Seasonality charts take an average of price movements at the same points in time historically and project the average forward to provide a possible roadmap of prices going forward
- Correlation between instruments should be plotted historically to understand if it is unusually high or low and how it is changing
- Log scale charts are best used for very long term charts or where prices have changed dramatically
- Flipping you charts upside down can help to remove any bias you might have
- The golden ratio can be used to project price retracements and price targets from a measured move in prices

# Chapter 5 - **Point and Figure Charts**

There are several different ways of representing price action on a chart. Nearly all the charts that we have looked at so far are simple line charts that join up the closing prices and plot a continuous line. There are a number of chart types that replace the line chart with forms of representation in order to show an extra level of information. In this chapter we will look at one such chart, the Point and Figure chart.

First, let's look at some other variations on the simple line chart. Bar charts join the high and low prices for the day as a vertical bar and then show the open and close as points marked on the left and right sides of the bar respectively. Bars can also be colour-coded for up and down days, as shown on the chart below. These give you a feel for the volatility in the price with the height of each daily bar. You can also see gaps between trading days that wouldn't show up on a line chart. We will look this in the next chapter.

Chart 5-1: Bar chart of Eurodollar

Other chart types include; wave charts, swing charts, Renko and Kagi charts and CBOT Market Profile charts, which are beyond the scope of this book. Cloud Charts are a new type of chart, and Candlestick charts, covered in the next chapter, are an integral part of these. Here we will see that Point and Figure charts are also a unique area of technical analysis.

It is impossible within the scope of this book to cover the subject of Point and Figure charts to a level where you can use them extensively. To really master this truly powerful technique The Definitive Guide to Point and Figure by Jeremy du Plessis is really the 'must read' on the subject. This section would not be possible without du Plessis's comprehensive book. A large number of technical analysts disregard this type of chart in the belief that it won't add any value to their work. This is a big mistake because Point and Figure Charts can add an extra dimension to your technical analysis in ways that no other technique can. We will come to see throughout this book how Cloud Charts and Point and Figure Charts frequently confirm one another. The more tools that point to the same outcome, the more you can trust that analysis for your trading decisions.

Point and Figure charts have a number of variations, but here we will just look at the popular three box reversal chart. The main reasons why all technicians should use these charts to aid their analysis are:

- Unambiguous breakouts show up for buy and sell signals
- Objective trends are defined much earlier than on other charts
- Reliable price targets are projected on the charts
- Clear Risk Reward Ratios are easily calculated
- Patterns and indicators used on line charts can be applied

Before we look at the really powerful features such as price targets it is necessary to understand how the charts came about and to learn their construction.

## Point and Figure construction

To get an understanding of how Point and Figure Charts are constructed it is best to look back to their origins. The charts were used by traders over a century ago, who didn't have the benefit of the data capture technology that we now take for granted. Recording every single price change and plotting graphs on big sheets of paper was also too onerous for traders, who were observing price changing either on chalk blackboards or via punched holes on a ticker tape machine over telegraph. Traders had to be quick to record prices that were not stored anywhere. Rather than record every price, market participants resorted to noting only the major changes or new units. The diagram on the left below shows how each new distinct price unit was recorded. If prices started at $17 and moved to $18½, 18 would be marked in the grid. If prices reversed, as we see happening here in the first column at $24, a new column would be started with each lower whole number recorded. Once prices stopped and started going back up again (here at $20, back through $21) a new up column would be started. This number grid was then simplified to the diagram we had on the left. This turned out to be a great shorthand for traders as they only had to enter a X (when prices were rising) or a O (prices falling) in a new 'box' with each new whole number at the start of the price.

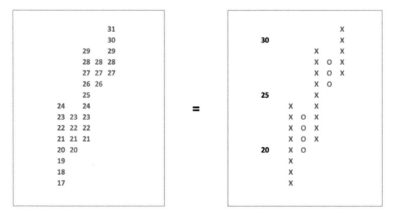

Figure 5-1: Point and Figure construction

Apart from reducing the work by recording only the important price changes, Point and Figure Charts effectively became a way of filtering out unwanted noise. The original one box reversal charts were increasingly considered as too sensitive around the 1930s and the three box reversal chart became more popular thereafter. This chart still favoured each incremental change in the direction of the column, but required a reversal through a full three increments for a new column to be started. At this point three X's or O's would be recorded. This means that, for three box reversal charts, a column must contain no fewer than three boxes. You will often see three box Point and Figure charts (even on the most expensive market terminals) with columns containing less than three Xs or O's in a column. These charts are incorrectly constructed and therefore not to be trusted for any form of Point and Figure analysis.

At this point there are a few useful aspects to notice in the construction of the Point and Figure chart. Firstly, each incremental move with the trend is recorded, while a reversal requires three incremental moves to be recorded. This asymmetrical filter whereby the trend is favoured over a reversal is unique to Point and Figure charts and is in line with the idea of 'the trend is your friend'.

A major feature is that the x-axis on the chart is not a time axis. A new column starts with each reversal. This means that time is not reflected in the chart. Instead we have a picture of change. It is true that columns to the left occurred at an earlier time and the highest X or the lowest O on the last right hand column is the last change to a new box. On a line chart, if prices don't change but time elapses, a horizontal line is drawn. On the corresponding Point and Figure chart, the chart remains unchanged. Only significant changes are recorded. The fact that time is not reflected in the chart can be difficult to understand at first, but it is worth persevering. Time can be shown on the charts with various software tools. New months can be shown or date and price can be highlighted with labelling tools. Here we see each year shown at the base of the 10 x 3 gold chart ($10 box by 3 box reversal – ie a reversal is $30l) for the last 30 years. This alone highlights there were a lot of price reversals in the year 2008 and very few in the mid 1990s.

Chart 5-2: Point and Figure chart of Gold over 30 years

The chart below shows the equivalent line chart is noisier with every price move shown.

Chart 5-3: Line chart of Gold over 30 years

## Box size

Because Point and Figure charts don't have a time axis, it is easy to assume that they are unhelpful for shorter term time periods. This is far from true. Not only can intra-day or tick data be used, but the sensitivity of the box size can be changed to reduce the size of the

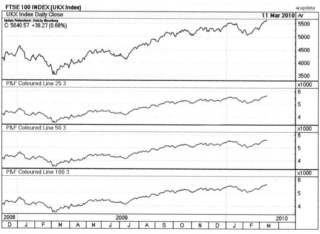

Chart 5-4: Line chart of FTSE 100 Index colour coded for different Point and Figure box sizes

noise filter. For instance if you are trading the UK FTSE 100 Index (Footsie) it is worth asking yourself the level of reversal you are prepared to live with. A shorter term trader may find a 150 point reversal (50 x 3 chart) to be unacceptable while a longer term trader will want to ignore such a move and stay with the bigger trend. The chart below shows a line chart colour coded for the columns you would see on Point and Figure charts of the same instrument. The box sizes of 25, 50 and 100 points are given in each window below the main chart respectively. The 100 x 3 chart in the bottom window shows only a handful of reversals in the last few years, while the 50 x 3 shows reversals coming in more frequently with more colour changes and the 25 x 3 shows even more.

Remember that a reversal is through full round increments in price. So with a 100 x 3 chart of Footsie, if the price had been above 5,500 a close below 5,200 points would be needed for a new column of O's to be started. It's not necessarily a 300 point reversal from a high or a low.

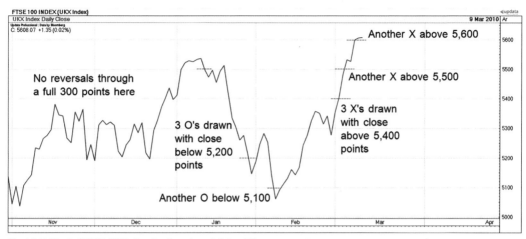

Chart 5-5: Chart of FTSE 100 Index showing where Point and Figure reversals occur

True Point and Figure charts are meant to be constructed from tick data. If the price moves into the new increment, with one price tick a new X or O would be recorded, depending on whether you are in an up or down column respectively. Storing years of tick data (millions of data points) in order to construct a heavily filtered chart is impractical. One way round this is to use the highs or lows each day in the price construction and for shorter term charts one minute data can be used instead. It is easy to forget that one day of one minute data is typically the equivalent of two years of daily data in terms of the number of data points. Below we see just a one day picture for Nymex Crude Oil with a sensitive 2.5c x 3 one minute chart. Intra-day charts like these are great for short term trading. We will cover this in more depth in Part 2 when we look at time horizon and using different techniques together.

As a rule of thumb, the ideal box size to start with is the nearest sensible number to one percent of the price for daily charts. So in the case of the S&P 500 Index at 1,150 points, a 10 x 3 chart would be the most sensible starting point, which means a reversal through 30 points (3 price increments) would force a column change.

Chart 5-6: Very short term intra-day chart of Oil with trends and price targets marked

## Buy and Sell signals

The patterns described earlier in this chapter also apply with Point and Figure charts, and while there are a few extra patterns, most patterns will boil down to a simple breakout at the end. One of the big advantages of Point and Figure charts is that breakouts are more clearly defined than with line charts. Below we see the most basic Point and Figure pattern 'a double top buy' signal. This is a little confusing as a double top pattern on a line chart would be like the pattern shown on page 38 in Chapter 2. The key thing with Point and Figure is that the price data is 'chunked' into the selected box size, such that the reversal has to be a 'pullback' in the price of at least the required magnitude (B) and then the breakout above the previous high (A) needs to occur by more than one full increment (C). As a result breakouts are clearly defined. Dow Theory of higher highs and lower lows is an integral part of Point and Figure charts with the added strength of the incremental box filter defining the extent to which pullbacks and breakouts in price need to occur. As a result the buy and sell signals are unambiguous.

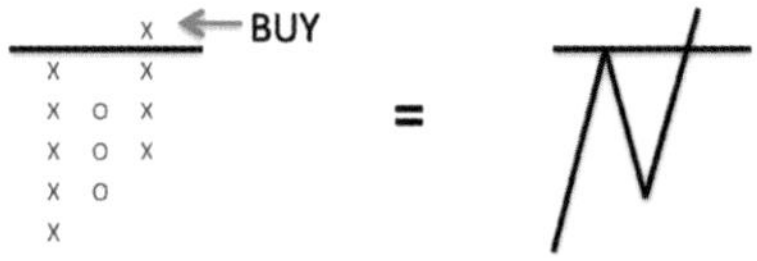

Figure 5-2: Double Top buy signal

As you would expect the reverse applies for double bottom sell signals.

Figure 5-3: Double Bottom sell signal

The triple top and bottom patterns are shown below. Here the resistance and support levels broken respectively are more established, so a bigger breakout is to be expected. But the double top and double bottom patterns are a subset contained within these patterns, so remembering those simpler patterns is enough to see buy and sell signals.

Figure 5-4: Triple Top and Triple Bottom signals

## Trend lines

Horizontal and subjective sloping trend lines can be drawn on a Point and Figure chart in the same way as on ordinary line charts as this chart connecting the low points shows below.

Chart 5-7: Subject trend drawn on AB Foods chart

But the truly powerful aspect of 3 box reversal Point and Figure charts is the ability to draw 45 degree lines off an extreme high or low on the chart. As we see in the chart below, this need not necessarily be the highest high or the lowest low on a chart. It often will be, but sometimes there is a 45 degree line to be drawn from a later turning point on the chart.

Chart 5-8: FTSE 100 Index with 45 degree trend line

When the 45 degree line is crossed a new countertrend line is drawn from the appropriate price extreme, normally low for a new uptrend or a high for a new downtrend. Price action below the downward sloping trend line is unequivocally bearish and price action above an upward pointing trend line is bullish. This unambiguous nature of trend state is a valuable aspect of Point and Figure charts which we will come to see is also present within Cloud Charts.

Chart 5-9: Kraft Foods with bullish and bearish trends

Another big advantage of the 45 degree trend lines is that they are far less retrospective than with line charts. Once a trend line is crossed a new trend 45 degree line off the appropriate high or low point is drawn. The trend is defined early on from a single price point and you don't have to wait for the price action to emerge, as you do with a line chart, in order to be able to draw the trend.

Here we see an example of the FTSE 100 Index where the trend became clear on the line chart around the point marked B.

Chart 5-10: Support line on FTSE 100 Index

That same point is marked on the corresponding Point and Figure chart below and here the trend was clear at A, which is also marked on the line chart above.

Chart 5-11: FTSE 100 Index with 45 degree trend line

Trends are often coming to an end by the time you can see them on a line chart. The earlier identification on a Point and Figure chart really helps with this dilemma. The direction of the last line drawn (projecting off the chart to the right) on a Point and Figure chart allows you to tell immediately whether a chart is bullish or bearish. There is no in between state. There is a similar attribute we find in Cloud Charts where the cloud off the right of the chart also immediately tells us the trend state. Point and Figure charts and Cloud Charts often confirm each other in this regard.

Whether you use line charts, Point and Figure charts or Cloud Charts, the price action often pulls away from the base trend. In the case of Point and Figure charts you can use internal lines to get an earlier warning to the trend reversing. This is another technical analysis risk reward conundrum. The earlier signal has a higher chance of failure versus the later signal, which will be much later and usually at a less favourable price. Looking at a smaller box size will also give earlier signals with higher sensitivity which is why it is always worth looking at more than one box size to get a better overall picture.

Chart 5-12: S&P 500 Index with trend lines including internal trend lines

## Signals with trend

With Point and Figure charts it is best to use the 45 degree trend lines as a filter for accepting or rejecting buy and sell signals. This simple idea ensures you trade with the prevailing trend and not against it. So when the price is running above the 45 degree uptrend you would be looking for each Point and Figure double top buy signal. When it is below the 45 degree downtrend you would be looking to take double bottom sell signals. There won't be many counter trend signals. As you would expect, buy signals are more common in uptrends and sell signals occur more frequently in downtrends. The main

Chart 5-13: FTSE 100 Index with signals aligned with trend marked

exception will be at the end of the trend when you start to get more countertrend signals, before the actual trend change is confirmed. Below we see a chart with the signals in line with the trends marked.

## Price Targets

By far the most alluring feature of Point and Figure charts is the generation of objective price targets, known as 'counts'. There are a number of different ways of calculating them which involve 'counting' columns or boxes. Horizontal counts were used on one box reversal charts over a hundred years ago, while vertical count targets were developed for 3 Box reversal charts in the late 1940s. Here we will only look at vertical count targets. To fully understand price targets, please refer to *The Definitive Guide to Point and Figure* book.

Point and Figure targets are about uninterrupted buying or selling thrust. There are four main situations where a vertical price target may be applied:

- An initial thrust off a low (or a high for a downside target)
- A second thrust off a low (or high) if the first move is very small (i.e. 3 X's or O's)
- A breakout column from a pattern
- Any long column that is clearly significant on the chart

Most columns in a Point and Figure chart are not countable under these rules. The price target is three times the length of any of these countable columns meaning the initial thrust is the first third of the potential overall price move. The longer this first thrust, the bigger the resultant move. The diagram below shows an example of the first rule of the ones listed above. With prices having fallen to new lows we see buying interest for the first time with a long column of X's off the low (A). This long column shows that we have 'uninterrupted' buying thrust. At no time during this first move off the low do we see enough of a pullback in price to create a reversal. This move may take some time. Point and figure does not take account of how long it takes, though this sort of thrust can occur quite quickly. The key thing is that at no time have the sellers come in to drive prices down enough to create a reversal. We do eventually get a reversal (B) which then 'locks' the thrust column and the target of a further two times the height of this column can be projected. The target is only activated with a move above the top of the first thrust column (here column C) which may be some time later. If price movement goes below the base of the column before thrust column then the upside target is negated and hence no longer valid, at which point it should be taken off the chart.

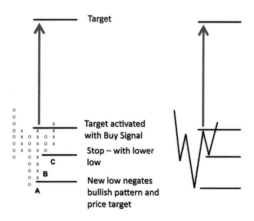

Figure 5-5: Point and Figure Vertical Count Target

It is important to note that targets are only approximate, though if you use them extensively you will come to realise that they can have an uncanny habit of being met exactly. If upside targets are met or exceeded, that is considered to be bullish confirmation and new upside targets can be taken more seriously. Failure to meet an upside target is a bearish sign. If downside targets are met or exceeded this is bearish confirmation while a failure to meet these targets would be a more bullish sign. Because there is no time axis on a Point and Figure chart there is no indication as to when a target will be met. It will not normally be in a single column as with the thrust column. The only way to get an idea of time horizon for a target is to refer to other time-based charts such as Cloud Charts. Point and Figure targets are the only precise rules-based price target system. This objectivity means that at all the trends and price targets can be placed on any chart with a simple key press on a computer. Other techniques such as price patterns or Fibonacci retracements and extensions require a degree of subjectivity in terms of where measured moves are taken from for price projection. Here we see examples of the vertical price target rules and the corresponding count targets.

Chart 5-14: FTSE 100 Index with vertical count targets of highs and lows

Chart 5-15: FTSE 100 Index with count from price thrust where first thrust was low

Chart 5-16: FTSE 100 Index with count from breakout column

Cloud Charts can also give target points where prices should find resistance and support as we will come to see. We will also look at using Cloud Charts and Point and Figure charts as a cross comparison for one another in .

## Multiple Price Targets

A price target's validity is increased if another target elsewhere points to the same target area. This may be two columns on the same chart pointing to the same target, or columns on charts of different box sizes that have thrusts pointing to prices arriving at the same place. This is why it is always worth starting with your rule of thumb of around one percent of the price for your first box size and then looking at sensible box sizes either side of this. For instance if you start with a box size of 10 points, it is worth exploring the 20 x 3 chart (longer term) and then the more sensitive 5 x 3 chart, and keeping a close eye out for clustering price targets across these charts. Below we see an example of targets clustering from two different thrust columns on the same chart.

Chart 5-17: BP with count targets clustering to same target price

There are often a number of price targets on a chart and it is important to remember that the nearest targets need to be met first, before getting too excited about the latest even bigger price targets. With trends it is quite often the case that a counter target is given before the trend has changed. You should wait for the trend change before relying on this counter trend target but the counter trend thrust is a warning sign. Similarly it is sometimes the case that the last target in a dying trend may not be met before the trend reverses. Furthermore, it is possible to have conflicting targets on a chart. In this case you should favour the target in the direction of the trend. Here we see such an example with the gold chart.

Chart 5-18: Natural Gas with upside and downside count targets

## Risk Reward Ratios

Because Point and Figure charts give you price targets and stop levels (i.e. a sell signal with a lower low) you can calculate risk reward ratios with each price target. Here we see Current Risk Reward (CRR) ratios for McDonald's Corp. These ratios are calculated as the distance from the current price to the target (i.e. 84.5 - 65.44) divided by the difference between the current price and the stop level of $63. The stop is where we would get a sell signal with a new O below the base of the previous column of O's. The ratio is calculated as 19.06/2.44. Risk Reward ratios are covered in more detail under Stop-losses and Money Management in Chapter 7.

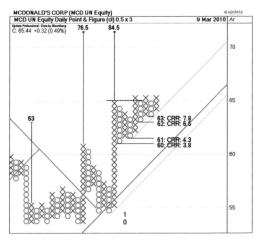

Chart 5-19: McDonald's with risk reward ratios

## Other indicators on Point and Figure charts

Many of the analysis techniques that you might use on line charts can be used on Point and Figure charts too. Here we see moving averages calculated on the average of previous column midpoints. So a 21 period moving average here looks back 21 columns for the rolling calculation. The averages work well here because they pull closer to the price and therefore give earlier signals than the 45 degree trend lines. It is worth noting that when prices have changed this dramatically, 45 degree trends will give very late signals. This chart also shows a histogram on the y-axis for volume at each price unit. This volume at a price level chart, rather than volume at a time on the x-axis with a line chart, can give a useful idea of the price levels where something is heavily traded.

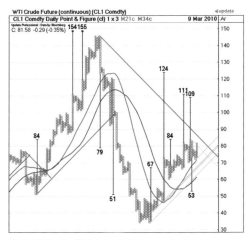

Chart 5-20: Oil with Point and Figure moving averages

Point and Figure log scale charts are also possible where the box size actually varies as a true percentage of the price. So here on this 1% x 3 chart of oil the box size would be 10 when oil was at $100 and 4 when oil was at $40. As a result the targets are rarely to whole numbers and invariably contain decimals. Oil will still be in a downtrend on the arithmetic $1 x 3 chart, as we saw in the previous chart. A log scale chart is appropriate here because of the dramatic changes in price in the last few years and as with the moving averages, can be used to get earlier signals. The log construction means that multiple targets are less likely to point to exactly the same price. In this example, the $87.16 and $88.03 levels are close enough to be considered a 'cluster'.

Chart 5-21: Log scale Point and Figure chart of oil

## Summary points

- There is no time axis on a Point and Figure chart – the x-axis shows number of reversals
- The box size defines the sensitivity of a Point and Figure chart
- Moves of one box are marked with the prevailing trend, three boxes against the trend for a reversal
- Unambiguous buy signals are given with a break above a previous up column (Xs)
- Unambiguous sell signals are given with a break below a previous down column (Os)
- Objective 45 degree trend lines define an unambiguous trend state
- Buy and Sell signals should be taken with the confirming trend and ignored countertrend
- Vertical price targets can be projected from appropriate thrust columns
- Targets pointing to the same price point (clustering) increases the likelihood of them being met
- Risk reward ratios can be calculated with targets and stops
- Other indicators and log scales charts can be used with Point and Figure charts

# Chapter 6 - **Candlestick Charts**

As outlined in the history of technical analysis in the first chapter of this book, Japanese technicians have been using Candlesticks for hundreds of years. They form an integral part of Cloud Charts and have been left to be covered towards the end of Part 1, in order to lead you into Cloud Charts in Part 2. Reading more about Candlestick Charts is highly recommended in order to get the most from Cloud Charts. It is impractical to cover every aspect of the Candlestick analysis in one chapter so here are the basics.

At the start of the previous chapter we explained the advantage that bar charts gave, over a single line chart, by showing the trading range of each day. Candlestick charts make these trading ranges clearer by showing the range between the highest price and lowest price for a day, as well as the range between the opening price and closing price for that day, in a more succinct way. Because candles assign more importance to the range between the open and the close, visually, with a wider body than bars, the four key elements of open, high, low and close on a trading day are much easier to see at a glance. While rising and falling bars may be colour coded as corresponding candles can, the wider body also allows candles to be further coded as hollow and solid, respectively. On days where the price closes higher than it opened, candles are hollow (often colour coded positively blue or green) and on days when the price closes lower than where it opened candles are filled solid (often colour coded negatively red or black).

A quick analogy for newcomers to remember is this, hollow candles are like balloons which go up and solid candles are like bricks which fall. The pictorial nuances of how candles represent price may not seem very important at this stage, but when it comes to recognising the various Candlestick price patterns it can be the difference between spotting them instantly, or missing them altogether. The almost subliminal information that candles can convey provides many traders with an extra dimension for decision making under pressure.

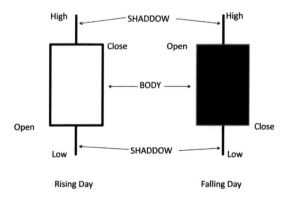

Figure 6-1: Candlestick elements

The candle representing a day's trading embodies the intra-day moves in price. Here we see two candles and how the tick price action over the day could correspond in each case. Once you are practiced at using candles you can start to visualise the intra-day trading behind each candle accordingly. Long spike-like shadows and small bodies highlight short term volatility, while tall bodies and no shadows indicate prices trending that day.

Figure 6-2: Possible price moves intra-day to match candle

Chart 6-1: Candlestick chart of Eurodollar

This Candlestick chart of the Euro above clearly shows up and down days.

The Dow Theory rules of higher highs and lower lows can be applied to individual candles on Candlestick Charts. The line diagrams we looked at on pages 31 and 32 in Chapter 2 could be represented by the candlestick charts for each day as shown below. The idea of higher highs and higher lows in an uptrend, and lower highs and lower lows are inherent in the highs and lows of each candlestick in relation to the previous day.

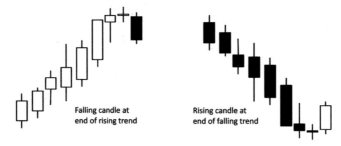

Figure 6-3: How candles can warn of the end of a trend

Candles can also lend pictorial value to trading in other ways that numbers on a screen can't. Here we see a market map of prices for a group of instruments with candles shown along side. It is much clearer from the candles where prices are in relation to their trading range for the day.

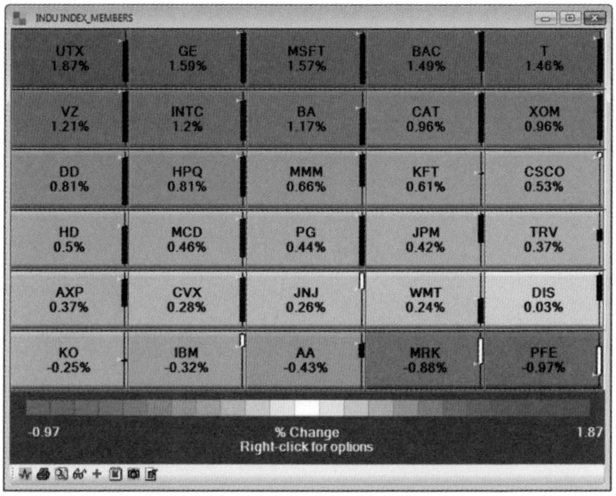

Figure 6-4: Market Map of the Dow Jones 30 stocks with candlesticks shown to the right of each stock code

## Gaps

Gaps occur on line and Candlestick charts when two consecutive days' trading ranges don't overlap in any way. Prices are said to have 'gapped up' or 'gapped down' when this happens and this is generally bullish and bearish respectively. But not all gaps are continuation signals with the trend. Gaps will also often provide support and resistance at a later date when prices return to these levels.

Chart 6-2: Alcoa chart with gaps marked

There are three common types of gap identified by western technicians:

- The breakaway gap occurs early on in a trend, often at the breakout stage from the patterns identified in Chapter 1. This confirms the sudden realisation that the uncertainty surrounding future price direction in a congestion zone is now over and a new trend has started. Breakaway gaps are the first clear gap in an uptrend or downtrend.
- Exhaustion gaps occur at the end of a trend when prices have one last spurt to an extreme point which cannot be sustained and is quickly reversed soon after. These gaps typically occur after a long uptrend or downtrend or when prices have run a long way up or down very quickly and the steepness of trend cannot be sustained.
- Continuation Gaps occur in the middle of the trend and there may be several small ones or one or two big one. They generally occur before the first half of the trend and often soon after a breakaway gap if there is one. You don't truly know if you have a continuation or exhaustion gap until you see the action of the next one or two candles. The extent of the trend is your clue and you may use other indicators to assess which scenario is most likely as well.

## Gaps and trading periods

We will look at time frames in a lot more detail in Chapter 10 in Part 2. There we will look at monthly, weekly and intra-day charts, but it is worth pointing out, here, that gaps are most likely to occur on daily and weekly charts. This is because of the overnight close and weekends in markets respectively. Gaps are less prominent on a monthly chart as they require that a daily one occurred by coincidence between the first and last day of the month, meaning none of the price action in adjacent months overlapped. Similarly, intraday charts are unlikely to have clear gaps, other than for overnight periods, because as one candle closes, another immediately opens. Gaps are also more likely to occur in charts of stocks and indices where the trading hours are more defined by clear market opening hours. Instruments such as currencies and commodities are less likely to contain gaps as they are traded globally across overlapping time zones each with a high degree of liquidity.

## Candlestick patterns

We looked at a number of price patterns in Chapter 2. Candlestick charts may also follow the patterns we see in line charts, but also add an extra dimension with unique Candlestick patterns which typically made up of one, two or three candles. Where these Candlestick patterns occur in relation to the prevailing trend is an important aspect of defining whether a pattern is a reversal or continuation pattern. Most patterns give an early warning of a reversal by identifying potential tops and bottoms using the candles. There are lots of patterns to learn for full mastery of Candlestick Charts. We will only cover the main ones in this chapter.

## Island Reversals

Island reversals are formed by 'marooned' single candles with gaps between both the previous and next trading day. You therefore don't know that you have one, until the close on the third day. They are counter trend signals that often highlight the extreme points of the trend. They are very easy to spot with the candles hanging out in space at the bottom or top of the price action, and one of the most valuable candle signals as a result.

Chart 6-3: Island reversal on Johnson & Johnson

## Doji

Perhaps the most famous Japanese single candle is the Doji. This is where the opening and closing prices are at the same level, or very close to one another. The shadow length may vary either side of the body, which is a horizontal line representing the equal levels of open and close. If the high and the low are the same distance from the open/close then this classic Doji, called a Rickshaw Man, represents the indecision of traders on the day. The Long Legged Doji, with longer shadows, is a good example of this. The Gravestone Doji is where the open and close line form a base, like a gravestone, making it easy to remember. It is a bearish candle showing the inability to hold on to the gains for a day, with prices ending back where they started, but it is really a counter trend signal after a series of trending candles. It is more likely to be at the top of a trend. The Dragonfly Doji occurs where the open/close line is at the high for the day. The spike down of the low means prices moved lower but came back up again demonstrating buying strength. The Dragonfly Doji is more likely to be at the end of a downtrend forming a bottom. These three Doji candles are shown below.

Figure 6-5: Candlestick Doji

## Stars

Where Doji (plural is the same as singular) occur in relation to the preceding trend in candles, is the key to interpreting them. If you see one after a good run in prices up or down, it signals new uncertainty and is called a Doji Star. A Star is a pattern where a candle with a short body gaps away from the body of the candle before it. The shadows of the two candles may overlap but the bodies don't. A Morning Star pattern is a bottom at the start up a new uptrend. You can remember this by morning signifying the sun is about to come out. An Evening Star (before darkness) signals the trend may be ending. The stronger Morning Star Doji and Evening Star Doji patterns occur when the bottom and top candle in the pattern are Doji. The Shooting Star, a top pattern, is where the extreme candle (called a Hammer, see below) has a high upper shadow, showing price exhaustion. These patterns are shown below.

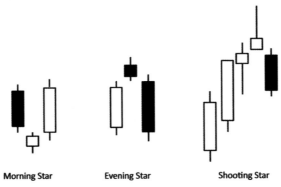

Morning Star          Evening Star          Shooting Star

Figure 6-6: Candlestick Star patterns

## Hammer and Hanging Man patterns

These patterns are formed where the body is small in relation to the full trading range, normally less than one third, and at one end of the range. The Hammer at the end of a downtrend signals that a reversal is imminent. The Hammer is 'hammering' out a base. The same shaped candle at the end of an uptrend is called a Hanging Man and signals the trend is slowing or reversing. An Inverted Hammer which, like a Hammer, occurs at a bottom and signals a reversal is effectively the opposite of a Shooting Star.

Figure 6-7: Hammer and Hanging Man patterns

## Engulfing patterns

Engulfing patterns should also be looked for at the end of a price trend. The bullish
engulfing pattern is where you have a hollow candle with a long body which 'engulfs' a
solid candle with a shorter body of the previous day. This is only meaningful after falling
prices, and with the fact that prices opened lower than the previous day's close and then
managed to close higher than the previous day's open. This shows buying strength which
should herald a new up move in prices. The bearish engulfing pattern is the reverse,
where, at the end of an uptrend, a large bodied down day candle overlaps a smaller up
day candle of the previous day at both ends. Here the price has opened higher than the
previous day's close, and then closed lower than the previous day's open, demonstrating
selling pressure and the likely end of the uptrend.

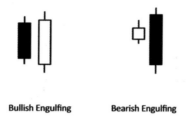

**Bullish Engulfing**     **Bearish Engulfing**

Figure 6-8: Engulfing patterns

## Harami patterns

Harami patterns appear as the opposite of engulfing patterns, but are still reversal
patterns, whereby the second candle body is smaller and overlapped at both ends by the
first candle. If the second candle is a Doji, the pattern becomes a Harami Cross and this is
a more powerful reversal pattern than a standard Harami. This pattern is significant on the
day of the Doji because the price range has been contained by the body of the previous
day, and, worse still, the price has closed right back where it started to form the Doji. The
Doji on its own shows indecision. The significance is increased at the end of a trend where
such indecision has not been prevalent.

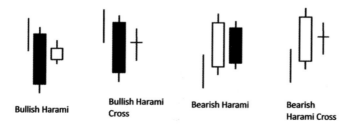

**Bullish Harami**     **Bullish Harami Cross**     **Bearish Harami**     **Bearish Harami Cross**

Figure 6-9: Harami Patterns

## Dark Cloud Cover and Piercing Patterns

These two patterns are also reversal patterns that can be easily recognised when a counter trend candle occurs at the end of a trend. It is the first clearly different candle in a series. The Dark Cloud Cover pattern is significant in that the open of the counter trend candle is higher that the high of the previous day, itself a strong up day, but then closes lower well within the body of the previous day. Initial buying strength on this day is heavily eroded, signalling a trend reversal. The piercing pattern is the reverse, at the end of a downtrend, with the extra requirement that price closes above the half way mark ('piercing it') of the previous body. In this case, prices opened lower than the previous trading day and then managed to close in the upper half of that trading range, showing buying strength at the end of a downtrend. It is interesting to note the use of the word 'cloud' in the naming of Japanese candle patterns hundreds of years before Cloud Charts where used.

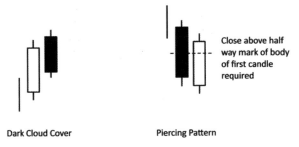

Dark Cloud Cover          Piercing Pattern

Figure 6-10: Dark Cloud Cover and Piercing Patterns

## Marubozu

These are abnormally big range trading days with no, or very little, shadow. The bullish Marubozu, sometimes called white (Yang) Marubozu, is where the price opens at the low for the day and closes much higher at the high for the day. This is a sign of real buying strength and is normally a sign of continuation in an uptrend. The bearish Marubozu (black - Yin) is a solid large down candle where the price has opened at the high for the day and closed much lower at the low. This shows real weakness with no buyers coming in at much lower prices. Marubozu will be instantly recognisable as the tallest candles on your chart with no spikes at ether end. The midpoint between the extremes of the Marubozu will often be a price level that serves as support (bullish Marubozu) or resistance (bearish Marubozu) at a later point in time.

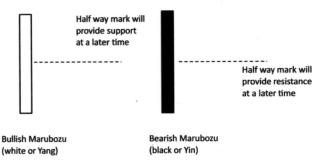

Bullish Marubozu          Bearish Marubozu
(white or Yang)           (black or Yin)

Figure 6-11: Marubozu

## Waiting a candle before trading

With daily charts, you cannot be certain of the pattern on the last candle until the market has closed. Given you are likely to have to wait until the market is open the following day, you are also left to see where the price opens that next day. The action of waiting is normally a good discipline to confirm the reversal pattern is valid. This sets you up well for knowing how you will trade the following day. You may decide to take the risk and trade earlier just before the close on the day of the pattern on the basis that you believe the pattern is about to be confirmed as you see it. One trading strategy is keener but riskier, the other is later and safer. It will come down to personal preference. We will explore the idea of a signal delay in the next chapter.

## Candlestick examples

The best way to get to grips with Candlestick patterns is to practice looking for them on your charts. Be aware that many of them will occur at the end of an uptrend or downtrend, so look for these anomalies which alert you to a likely change. You can easily scan for them or set most software systems to highlight the patterns on your charts on a computer screen. Here are a few real life examples of some of the patterns we have covered in this chapter.

Here we see a Morning Star Doji for Antofogasta

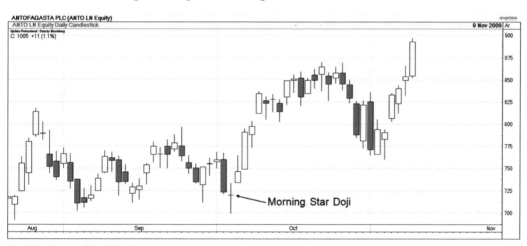

Chart 6-4: Morning Star Doji on Antofagasta

## Bullish Engulfing on Royal Dutch Shell

Chart 6-5: Bullish Engulfing patterns on Royal Dutch Shell

## Dark Cloud Cover on Pearson plc

Chart 6-6: Dark Cloud Cover on Pearson

## Other candle types

The main Candlestick patterns described earlier can help you to identify tops and bottoms more clearly by exposing the shorter term trading psychology occurring a day or two after a reasonably long trend. We have shown that candles are constructed, shaded and coloured using the open, high, low and close of each day. There are a number of other ways candles can be represented. Here are just a few, which we will also explore further with Cloud Charts in Part 3.

Heikin-Ashi candles calculate the candles differently by replacing the open, high, low and close values of normal candles as set out on the next page.

Close = (Open+High+Low+Close)/4

Open = (Open (previous bar) + Close (previous bar))/2

High = Max (High, Open, Close) – where Open and Close are those above

Low = Min (Low, Open, Close) – where Open and Close are those above

From this we see that the chart shows up the trend change much more clearly for oil giving you below a much better idea of when a downtrend ends and an uptrend starts.

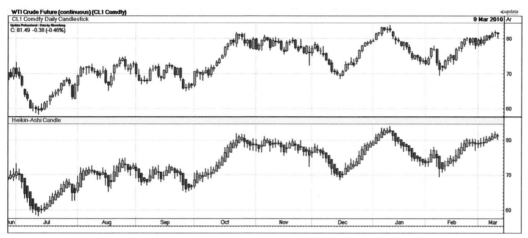

Chart 6-7

Candle Volume Charts incorporate volume into each candle on a chart by increasing their width proportionally to the volume on a given day. This means the time scale on x-axis is irregular. Each day's width and height on the chart now tells us more about demand. A short, wide candle means there is a lot of trading occurring with buyers and sellers fairly evenly matched. A tall thin candle shows prices are moving quite dramatically on low volume. These charts can help you to see volume increasing early on in the trend and decreasing as the trend nears an end. All the candle patterns covered in this still apply but with the added dimension of seeing if price moves are confirmed by volume. The candle volume chart of General Electric is shown below.

Chart 6-8: Candle Volume on GE

## Cloud Charts

Candlestick charts are an integral part of the Cloud Chart. This chapter should give you enough understanding to be able to recognise candlestick patterns when you come to use Cloud Charts. The chart below is a Cloud Chart of Boeing with some Candlestick patterns highlighted.

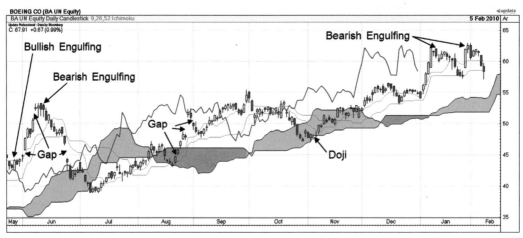

Chart 6-9: Cloud Chart of Boeing with candlestick patterns marked

## Summary points

- Candlesticks are shown as hollow on up days and solid on down days
- Gaps occur where there is no overlap in the trading range on the previous day
- Island Reversals are where a candle is marooned with gaps either side at a top or a bottom
- Doji at the end of a run in prices indicate indecision and a potential reversal
- A Morning Star after a downtrend signals the potential beginning of a new uptrend
- An Evening Star after an uptrend signals the potential beginning of a new downtrend
- Morning Star Doji and Evening Star Doji are stronger patterns
- Engulfing patterns are signalled by tall counter trend candles 'engulfing' a smaller candle
- Dark Cloud Cover and Piercing patterns are simple countertrend candles after a run in prices
- Marubozu are very tall candles where the midpoint may serve as support or resistance later
- It normally pays to wait a candle for the pattern to be confirmed
- Candles can be combined such as Heikin-Ashi
- Candle Volume Charts represent volume using proportionally wider candles
- The candlestick Chart is the normal way price is shown on a Cloud Chart

# Chapter 7 - **Using Stop-losses**

In this chapter we will look at maximising your trading profits with stop-losses. Money management is a vital part of successful long term investing or shorter term trading. Understanding how to trade with stop-losses will also be useful when we look at similar cloud stop techniques.

## The maths are against you

When most people start out trading, they don't appreciate that there is an inbuilt mathematical disadvantage to trading. Percentage loss and percentage gain from a starting point are not equal going forward. For instance if you lose 10% of your capital on a trade you are left with 90% of your original capital, and to get back to where you were on the next trade you need more than a 10% gain. A 10% return on the 90% you are left with will in fact be 9% of your previous capital. If you had a losing 10% trade and a winning 10% trade, you will therefore have ended up losing 1% overall. The same applies if your trades are the other way round. If you win 10% on your 100% first, you get to 110% of your original capital, and if you then lose 10% of that amount it will be the equivalent of 11% of your original capital taking you to 99%. Either way round a winning trade of 10% and a losing trade of 10% will end up costing you 1%. Percentage losses cost more than percentage gains.

The next aspect of losses versus gains is that the cost increases exponentially. If you lose 20% of your capital and then make 20% on your new capital pool, you are left with 96% of your starting capital, not the 98% you might expect from the previous 10% exercise. Indeed, if you lose 20% of your capital, you need 25% (20 upon 80) to get back to where you were. If you lose a third, you need a 50% return on what you have left to recover the third lost. Lose half and you need to double your money next time and so on. This burden of recovery is what encourages gamblers to take bigger risks in attempt to win back money they have lost. The more you lose, the more you need to win to get back to where you were. The table inset in the chart below highlights this in numerical terms and as we see from the chart, lose more than half your money in a trade and it becomes an impossible road to recovery.

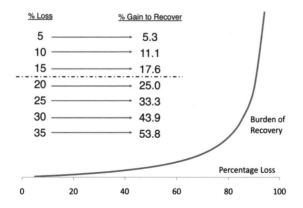

Figure 7-1: Why percentage losses outweigh percentage profits

Keeping your losses small is an essential part of a successful trading strategy. Furthermore, it is this aspect of a trade over which you have the most control. No matter what trading technique you use to enter a trading position in a given market, you have no real control over how successful that trade will be. We have seen that there are tried and tested tools you can use to increase the probability that you are entering a trade at an ideal price, but the reality is, you cannot control how prices change from that point. The market does not care where you bought and the picture can change from the one you predicted. Some trades go better than expected, but often you won't do as well as you hoped. Even the most successful traders have to live with losses. Once you have entered a trade, the only thing you can truly control thereafter is how much money you are prepared to lose. You might be lucky enough to control your profits on winning positions, but more often than not you will be dealing with the worry of taking losses. Losses need to be controlled.

So we see the need to come up with a strategy that primarily keeps losses smaller, but is also not detrimental to making good profits when they are available. Stop-losses are based on four golden rules of trading:

1. Cut your losses
2. Cut your losses
3. Cut your losses
4. Let your profits run

## The Trailing Stop-loss

The idea behind the trailing stop-loss is simple. First a percentage (or number of points) representing a small fraction of the price of an instrument is set below the price such that it provides a price exit level or stop. With a trailing stop, the stop level rises (trailing the price) when the price rises and moves sideways when the price falls back from a peak. The trailing stop can only start rising again when the last high (where the trailing stop started to move sideways) is exceeded. The chart below shows a 10% stop-loss for the S&P 500 Index.

Chart 7-1: Trailing 10% stop-loss on S&P 500 Index

## Best Fit Stop-losses

The trailing stop-loss worked quite well on this chart above but 10% will not be the best level to use on every chart. For instance this chart of the Dow Jones Index below shows 10% was giving too much away. The 5% level is too tight as it gave a sell signal in the summer pullback of 2009. The best fit percentage in this case is 8%.

Chart 7-2: 'Best fitting' stop-loss for Dow Jones Industrial Average

This technique of 'best fitting' the percentage is similar to the idea of curve fitting the periods with moving averages we discussed on page 52. Like averages, stop-losses can also be applied to charts derived from the price line, such as relative strength, equally well. Stop-losses can also be set for trading short positions whereby the stop-loss only falls when prices fall, and the stop-loss is then drawn above the price. On the chart below, we see a short stop-loss on a relative strength chart of EDF Group.

Chart 7-3: Short stop-loss on relative strength chart of EDF Group

By setting the stop-loss to best fit price retracements within a trend we are aiming to establish the difference between a normal pull back in the price within the trend and an 'abnormal retracement'. But retracements in the trend may not be constant and may become smaller as the trend progresses. Each successive pullback in the price provides you with a new level of information to set a tighter stop-loss. We see this in the chart of Gold below.

Chart 7-4: Gold chart with tightening stop-losses

If prices start to run up very quickly as we see here with this chart of copper, then tightening the stop is the only way to catch the end of the trend near the top. With this sort of chart, most forms of analysis will not be of help.

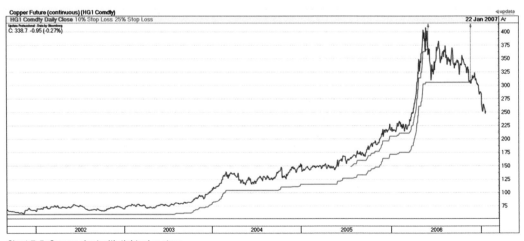

Chart 7-5: Copper chart with tightening stops

## Optimised Stop-losses

Most traders will be looking for the shorter term trends to trade within the longer term trend and this is where computer optimised stop-losses come into their own. An algorithm or tool, such as an RSI, can be used to establish low points and then a series of iterations run from these lows to find the optimum percentage stop-loss to use in the resulting short term trends. The Optimised Stop-loss works out the most money that can be made over a chosen time through this process of optimisation. Here we see the shorter term trades marked on the oil chart below using such a process. The success of the trades in this example rests more heavily on trading with the trend and choosing the right stop-loss percentages than it does about getting your entry right. Evidence from back-tests suggests that a good money management system such as optimised stop-losses with randomly selected entry points will win over a system which picks every low perfectly, with poor money management.

Chart 7-6: Medium term and long term trading stop-losses for Oil

Many traders complain about getting 'stopped out' when the price quickly rises back up through their stop-loss. By optimising the stop-loss to fit normal price behaviour, temporary breaches should occur much less frequently. But even if you sell on an arbitrary stop-loss being breached, the last thing you remember is that the price went back up above the level you sold at.

What often transpires is that the price goes on to make a lower high (Dow Theory) before falling back through the stop level where you sold to make new lower lows. Here we see this a number of times on the chart of the Microsoft below.

Chart 7-7: Optimised Stop-losses for Microsoft

## Temporary breaches of Stop-losses

Situations where the price falls temporarily below an important level are common in most areas of technical analysis. Support and resistance levels will see such breaches and they can occur frequently on Cloud Charts as well. With stops the breach is amplified because it normally involves a trading decision and this often involves crystallising a trading loss.

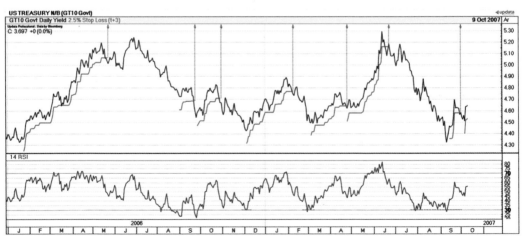

Chart 7-8: US Treasury Bonds with stop-losses and RSI

When faced with a breach of a stop, there are a few things you need to remember. Firstly, the current bar for the time series used needs to be locked by the close for the signal to be truly given. It may prove valuable to wait an extra bar or two before taking a stop-loss breach as a signal. As we saw with Candlestick charts, waiting until just before the end of the period before accepting a signal is one strategy. This does not allow for the fact that prices may open above the stop-loss on the next day but it does deal with the risk of the price opening much lower once a stop has been breached. The number of days to wait after a signal is given for confirmation can also be optimised and up to three bars may prove optimal. This 'signal delay' mechanism is one of the best ways to deal with 'whipsaws' in the price line. The last chart shows the US 10 year Treasury bond. Optimisation of the signal delay shows that it generally pays to wait a day before exiting.

While the price may demonstrate a characteristic of bouncing back briefly after a stop breach, it can be dangerous to wait if it doesn't do so quickly, so long signal delay periods are not recommended. With an optimised stop-loss abnormal retracements are being identified based on previous price history. When the price is below the stop, the risk of sharp falls in price is increased. The longer the price sits below a stop, such that it is now not a spike, the greater the level of risk that bigger falls are about to occur. But it also pays not to be too eager to exit on a temporary breach. It is generally best to find a happy medium of waiting one or two days (or bars) depending on your trading style.

The chart below shows how UBS made the first intra-day breach of its long term optimised stoploss at A. The extent of the shadow of this first breaching candle gave a measure for subsequent breaches. At B the shadow below the stop is of much the same extent but the price manages to close above the stop. At C the shadow is well below the levels set at A and B and the price even closes at the level of A & B. At this point, heading into the close, with no realistic chance of a close above the stop the trader may decide to exit. At candle D, the price opens lower still but not much lower. Either way at both C and D the price is in fundamentally different territory than A & B. One point to note, is that, if the stop-loss has been running sideways for longer than usual, the risk of bigger falls is increased by the fact that the 'spike' down in price longer is than usual.

Chart 7-9: UBS chart with stop-loss

## Sideways moves and exit guarantee

Stop-losses deal with price moment in two important ways, where many other indicators fail. As we have seen prices can spend long periods consolidating, moving sideways, while indicators continue to oscillate giving signals. Stop-losses set at the right percentages will handle this sideways translation in price and keep you in the trade for the next big move. Stop-losses are also a guaranteed exit on the price and you may not get an exit on an indicator derived from the price at all. The signals for entry on the chart on page 110 were generated with a short term RSI. The RSI is normally read as rising through 30 for a buy and falling through 70 as a sell. The exit signals in this example were given with the optimised stoploss. When the trades were long and profitable you generally got an RSI exit falling through 70. But when the trades didn't work out, the RSI, having given buy signals at 30, did not make it to 70 in order to give corresponding sell signals. Had you relied on the RSI you would not have had a signal to sell at all.

Your exit signals should always be based on the price, as price is the true measure of your profit and loss account. Most indicators run the risk of not giving you a guaranteed exit and tools such as moving averages will often be too slow. Using support and resistance along with the price patterns set out in Chapter 2 is one strategy for exiting, but it is often too subjective. Point and Figure charts give more objective signals and we will see that Cloud Charts give exit signals as well. But optimised stop-losses have the advantage of being very simple to read and can be tightened when prices move dramatically, helping you to run profits further and get out closer to the top (or bottom if you are in a short trade). The other reason you should consider using them as your exit tool, over any other technique, including Cloud Charts, is that it is a very good discipline to use a different form of technique to get you out of a trade, than the one that got you in. This will save you from convincing yourself that your original analysis on entering a trade is still right.

## Risk Reward Ratios and position sizing

We looked briefly at risk reward ratios in the chapter on Point and Figure charting. Because of the unique targets and stops you get on a Point and Figure chart, it is possible to have these calculated automatically on your charts. You can do this subjectively with stop-losses as well, to establish whether the trade has the right level of profitability to justify the downside risk. You can use other forms of analysis to arrive at price targets such as price patterns or Fibonacci. Once you have established your price target level for a trade and your optimised stop-loss, you can calculate your risk reward ratio. The ideal trade is where the profit (target) outweighs the downside risk (stop) by a ratio of 3 to 1.

This applies for both upside targets with downside stops, and downside targets with short upside stops. The simple diagram below highlights the optimum risk reward ratio. Remember while these ratios are called 'risk reward' they are actually calculated as reward divided by risk.

Figure 7-2: Calculating Risk Reward Ratios

Even if you cannot clearly establish your upside price target for a trade you wish to make, your percentage stop-loss will help you ascertain whether a trade is viable. If your stop is tight you don't need a lot of upside to make the trade work. Once you have established your optimum stop at, say, 5%, ask yourself can you really see 15% upside? If your risk reward ratio is only 2 to 1, consider taking a smaller position. If it is 4 or 5 to 1, the trade might be too good to be true. If the ratio is 1 to 1, ask yourself why you are prepared to trade when the upside and the downside are equal.

You should also consider your position sizing if the percentage stop is smaller or wider than usual. You can assign more of your capital to a trade with narrower stops and favourable risk reward ratio, while a wider stop than normal should alert you to placing a smaller trade.

## Parabolic SAR

Another stop-loss tool which has similar money management characteristics to the optimised stop-loss is the Parabolic SAR invented by J. Welles Wilder. This produces a stop and reverse trading system where the signals are generated using a weighted moving average, but with the weighting favouring the more recent prices using an acceleration factor as the trend progresses. This factor can also be optimised for the best overall profit results. Due to the acceleration in the calculation, the Parabolic SAR, normally drawn as dots, accelerates towards the price. This gives you the built in effect of tightening up your stops automatically which optimised stop-losses fixed at a percentage don't do.

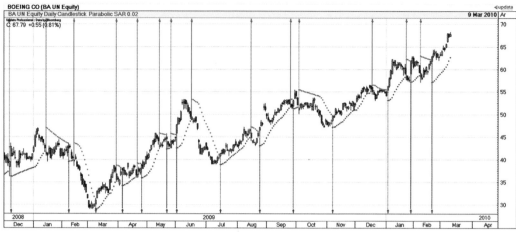

Chart 7-10: Parabolic SAR for Boeing

The same stop and reverse idea used for Parabolic SAR can be applied to optimised stop-losses. Here we see a chart of Boeing with a custom programmed 'flip-flop' stop-loss which has been optimised to give the most profit for this instrument over the last three years. The stops on this chart swap from long to short as shown and an equity line of trading profits using this strategy is shown.

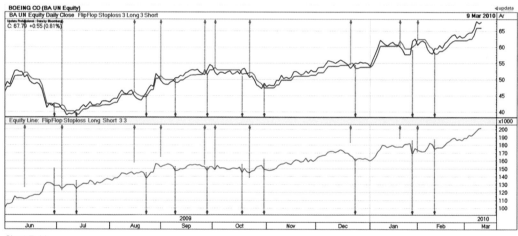

Chart 7-11

We will look at back-testing and optimisation of Cloud Charts in Part 3, but it is interesting to see how these stop and reverse systems rank alongside trading other analysis tools already covered in this book. These tests were run on a series of 24 currency pairs on daily data over a period. What the table below highlights, is that money management tools, such as Optimised Stop-losses and Parabolic SAR's produced better overall returns, but with a win/loss ratio of 1. The gains were 3 to 1 as a result of keeping losses small. The systems at the bottom table had better win to loss ratios, but the losses and the gains were the same. Remember we identified losses had a bigger impact than gains at the start of this chapter. Keep your losses small and your trading profits will not be eroded.

| | Trades | Equity | % Profit | Draw Down | Ave Profit | Max Gain | Max Loss | Gain/ Loss | No. Wins | No. Loss | Win/ Loss |
|---|---|---|---|---|---|---|---|---|---|---|---|
| Flip Flop Stoploss | 100 | 16045 | 60 | 330 | 67 | 936 | 304 | 3 | 51 | 48 | 1 |
| Parabolic SAR | 116 | 15267 | 53 | 300 | 46 | 920 | 334 | 3 | 57 | 58 | 1 |
| Directional Movement | 162 | 14589 | 46 | 253 | 29 | 935 | 278 | 3 | 82 | 78 | 1 |
| Exponential Moving Averages | 102 | 14129 | 41 | 399 | 47 | 797 | 328 | 2 | 51 | 50 | 1 |
| Bollinger Bands | 54 | 13784 | 38 | 998 | 98 | 632 | 650 | 1 | 36 | 16 | 2 |
| RSI | 25 | 13275 | 33 | 1275 | 217 | 805 | 607 | 1 | 18 | 7 | 3 |
| Commodity Channel Index | 88 | 13214 | 32 | 990 | 47 | 567 | 717 | 1 | 56 | 27 | 2 |

Figure 7-3: System Test Results – 'Flipflop' Stop-loss

Optimised stop-losses do have a failure rate whereby you would have been better to stay in the trade at a later point. Back-tests suggest the failure rate is around 20%. All techniques have a failure rate, but the bigger question is 'what is the failure?' With stop-losses it is a lost profit opportunity. With many other techniques the failure can be a loss of capital.

## Summary points
- The maths are against you – losses cost more than gains
- Long trailing stop-losses only move higher when prices make new highs
- Short trailing stop-losses only move lower when prices make new lows
- Stop-losses can be 'best fitted' to retracements within the trend for a given instrument
- Optimised Stop-losses are calculated for maximised profits via a series of iterations
- Signal Delays help deal with whipsaws in price and can also be optimised
- Optimised Stop-losses can keep you invested with sideways moves in price
- Stop-losses are a guaranteed exit based on the price
- Stop-losses help you understand Risk Reward Ratios for position sizing a trade
- Parabolic SAR is an effective 'stop and reverse' trading system
- Back-tests show that good money management has the biggest effect on profits

# Part 1 Summary

The preceding chapters are by no means a complete summary of the subject of Technical Analysis. There are many more comprehensive textbooks covering the techniques outlined as well as other areas not covered. There are complete books dedicated to the subject material in each chapter, which are referenced in the Bibliography at the back of this book. But if technical analysis is new to you, and you have read the first part of the book, you should now have all you require to get started in understanding Cloud Charts and be able to apply them in combination with other techniques. No one technical analysis technique on its own will give you everything you need to project the direction of future prices. The more tools you have in your tool-kit the better you will be able to do the job. Some tools may be used more frequently or prove more valuable than others at certain times and in the end a lot of it will come down to personal choice. The main thing is that tools do not sit in the bottom of the toolbox because you don't know how or when to use them. It is worth practising using all the techniques covered in Part 1 to improve your overall ability to analyse financial markets.

## What we have learned

Technical Analysis is a highly developed form of financial analysis that has been used by traders in the Eastern and Western Worlds for centuries. The basic tenets of Dow Theory, developed nearly one hundred years before computers, still hold true regarding how prices behave in the fast moving markets of today.

A key part of technical analysis is using tools to establish the prevailing trend in prices. We have the basic patterns in price to help us understand when the trend might be starting or when it might be coming to an end. By being able to determine levels of price resistance and price support we have a better idea of where prices will stop rising and where they should stop falling respectively.

We have discovered that patterns in price can be used to determine how prices are likely to move in the future. We have learned how to identify patterns of consolidation before the trend continues and when the trend is reversing.

Moving averages, constructed from a rolling average of prices, also assist with trend definition. We have looked at the various signals from crossovers and a number of techniques for arriving at the best look-back period to use. These same techniques can be applied to indicators.

Indicators can guide us in terms of what might be about to happen to prices, by looking at rates of change of speed and acceleration. With customised and programmed indicators there is potentially an infinite number of ways to analyse price behaviour. Divergence between price and indicators is a common theme that we covered in Part 1, and which we will revisit in Part 3.

It is possible to look at relationships between different instruments using relative strength and spread charts and we have seen that technical analysis tools can be applied to these charts as well. Seasonality can be taken into account in a chart, along with a host of other factors. Chapter 4 showed how the historical correlation relationship between different instruments can be studied to understand how strongly they are influencing one another at a given time, and whether that influence is increasing or decreasing. We also looked at flipping charts to remove bull or bear side bias and price retracement tools.

Point and Figure Charts were covered in Part 1 to build understanding when we come to compare this powerful technique with Cloud Charts in Part 2. The brief descriptions of their construction, the buy and sell signals, objective trends and price targets should provide enough of a background to using these charts. To master them further reading is needed.

Candlestick Charts were the last chart type we covered. These are the base chart in the Cloud Chart. We looked at gaps and the main candle patterns so that they can be identified on a Cloud Chart. As with all techniques, practice is needed. Candlestick Charts are no exception. If you can learn the patterns shown in Chapter 6 off by heart, you will see them time and time again on Cloud Charts.

Finally, we looked at stop-losses and money management, because, no matter how good your analysis, if you fail to grasp the importance of capital preservation while trading you are unlikely to be successful. This chapter will stand you in good stead when we look at cloud breaches and Cloud Stop-losses.

# Part 2 - **Understanding Cloud Charts**

---

*"A cloud does not know why it moves in just such a direction and at such a speed... It feels an impulsion... this is the place to go now. But the sky knows the reasons and the patterns behind all clouds, and you will know, too, when you lift yourself high enough to see beyond horizons."*

Jonathan Livingston Seagull, Richard Bach 1936 -

# Chapter 8 - **Cloud Chart Construction**

Cloud Charts look complex at first glance and there is some irony in this as 'Ichimoku' in Japanese is often translated as 'at a glance.' Once you do get the hang of these charts it is true that you will start to see a lot of information at a glance. There are a number of key elements on the chart and we will look at each of these in turn. Cloud Charts are very simple to construct because all the lines are derived purely and simply from the price history alone. There are five lines that make up a Cloud Chart:

1. Turning Line (sometimes called Conversion Line)
2. Standard Line (sometimes called Base Line)
3. Cloud Span A (sometimes called Cloud Span 1)
4. Cloud Span B (sometimes called Cloud Span 2)
5. The Lagging Line (sometimes called Lagging Span)

These lines are shown on the chart below

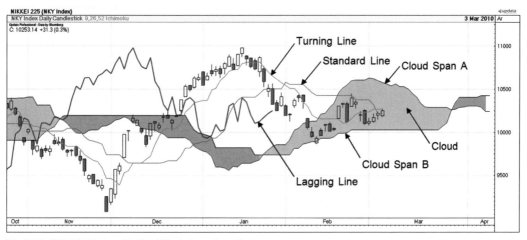

Chart 8-1: Nikkei 225 Index with Cloud Chart elements marked

## Turning Line

Sometimes called the conversion line, this line is constructed like a moving average. The look back period is 9 days, but instead of averaging each day in the period, we are calculating the overall midpoint between the highest daily high and the lowest daily low in the period.

This is the midpoint of the trading range across the last nine days. Take the highest price and the lowest price in the last nine days, add them together, divide by two and you have the plot for the turning line. Do this for the next day, now omitting the day 10 days ago which was in the last calculation, plot and so on. The chart below shows this.

Chart 8-2: Chart showing how the plot for the turning line is calculated

The pink line on the chart below shows how the turning line looks

Chart 8-3: How the turning line is plotted

The next chart compares the turning line with a 9 day moving average. Notice how the moving average line is smoother. This is because 9 days are added up and divided by 9 to give the plot. For the turning line, it is quite often the case that the plot is the same the next day. If the high or low used in the calculation occurred less than nine days ago, the turning line will not change on the next day. It is these sideways periods or 'steps' that make the turning line look more jerky than a moving average.

The turning line may be read as you would read a moving average but, with all the other elements in a Cloud Chart, it is unlikely that you will read this line and the price crossing each other. The 9 day period comes from one and a half times the original six day Japanese trading week. This is the first line in the construction of the Cloud Chart.

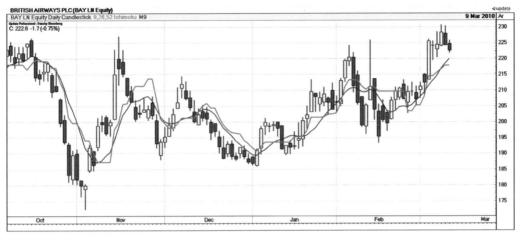

Chart 8-4: The turning line compared to a 9 day moving average

## Standard Line

This line, sometimes called the base line, is calculated in exactly the same way as the turning line but with a look back period of 26 days, originally the number of Japanese trading days in a typical month or 4 and a bit trading weeks. Below we see the standard line compared with a 26 day moving average. Because of the longer look back period, meaning the line can run sideways for longer, the standard line looks even more jerky than the turning line when compared with a moving average of the same period.

Chart 8-5: The standard line compared to the 26 day moving average

The turning and standard lines may also be read like moving averages. The easy way to remember which is which is by the fact the turning line is the shorter period of the two because it 'turns' more often. As the 9 day average snakes about the 26 day average, the turning line turns about the standard line. The chart below compares the turning line and the standard line in the top window and the 9 and 26 day moving averages in the bottom window. The top chart has the moving average signals marked on to allow a comparison. At point A the signals for both charts occur around the same place. At B the moving average signal was given a couple of days earlier, while at C it was given a few days later. We will look at when signals given with these two lines are most useful later in this chapter.

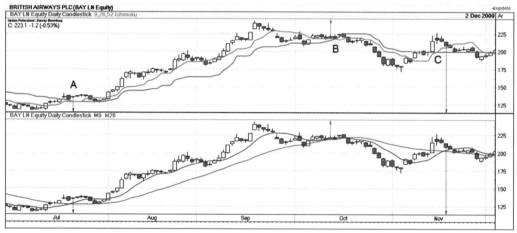

Chart 8-6: Turning and standard lines compared to 9 and 26 day averages

## Constructing the Cloud

The turning and standard lines serve a more valuable purpose than simply showing the lines themselves when it comes to Cloud Charts. The cloud is made up of two lines called spans. The first span of the cloud is the midpoint between the turning line and the standard line, but shifted 26 bars forward as shown.

Chart 8-7: Calculation of Cloud Span A

Translating a line forward in time in this fashion is a unique aspect of Cloud Charts and key part of the value they bring to technical analysis, which we will come to see. The second span is not related to either the turning line or the standard line but is produced in a similar way. Here we take the midpoint of the last 52 (2 trading months) sessions and shift it 26 bars forward in the same manner as with span A. In the chart below, we can see how we arrive at a point for span B on a given day.

Chart 8-8: Calculation of Cloud Span B

The spans that form the cloud are similar to 17 day (midpoint of 9 and 26) and 52 day averages shifted forward. The chart below shows the spans (shifted) and averages (also shifted) to give an idea of this. It is always worth remembering that the cloud is formed from a shorter term and a longer term average snaking around one another, which is shifted ahead of the price.

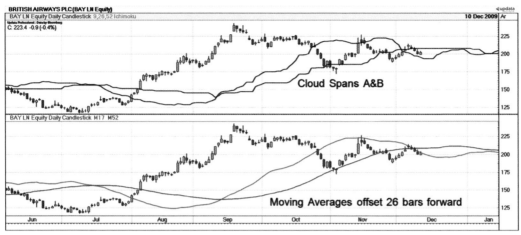

Chart 8-9: The cloud compared to moving averages

The area between the spans (the cloud) is normally shaded or hatched with lines, as below, on most professional market terminals.

Chart 8-10: The cloud for British Airways, hatched

You may prefer to use full shading instead. The cloud is normally colour-coded, depending on where the lines are in relation to each other. Remember, the cloud spans behave just like a shorter term and longer term moving average. If the shorter term span A is above the longer term span B, then prices are running up faster in the short term than they are longer term. This is bullish, and the cloud in this case is shaded in blue.

If prices are falling faster in the short term, this is bearish, and the cloud is red here. Generally the bullish (blue) cloud will be rising and the bearish (red) cloud will be falling.

Chart 8-11: The cloud for British Airways, Shaded

## Lagging Line

The lagging line, sometimes called the lagging span, is the fifth and final line on a cloud chart. The lagging line crossing the cloud is the 'confirming' signal in cloud chart analysis. This line is constructed simply by shifting the price line back 26 sessions. The thing to remember about Cloud Chart construction is the cloud is shifted forward 26 bars and the lagging line is shifted back 26 bars.

Chart 8-12: The Lagging Line offset from the price

The lagging line effectively interacts with a 52 session midpoint of itself (cloud span B) 52 sessions ago. The chart below depicts the lagging line and cloud span B. We will come to see that these two lines crossing is normally the major signal on a Cloud Chart.

Chart 8-13: The Lagging Line and Cloud Span B

The construction of the Cloud Chart is summarised as follows:

1. Turning Line - midpoint of the high and low of the last 9 sessions
2. Standard Line - midpoint of the high and low of the last 26 sessions
3. Cloud Span A - midpoint of turning line and standard line shifted 26 bars forward
4. Cloud Span B - midpoint of high and low of last 52 sessions shifted 26 bars forward
5. The Lagging Line - the price line (close) shifted back 26 bars

## Putting it all together

Even having learned the simple construction, Cloud Charts do look noisy to begin with and it is worth spending some time configuring your charts so you can read them more clearly. For instance many systems colour-code candle stick charts blue or green (rising), and red (falling). If your clouds are colour coded similarly or your shading isn't heavy enough such that the cloud is not so clear, you may consider reconfiguring your colours.

Chart 8-14: Chart of Dow Jones Index configured with hatched cloud

The chart below is the same as the one above with the candles coloured black, the cloud more heavily shaded and span B set to a higher thickness to highlight a cross of the cloud. The lagging line is drawn thicker than the standard and turning lines to highlight it. You may find this configuration clearer, or have another preference.

Chart 8-15: Chart of Dow Jones Index configured with shaded cloud

You may even decide not to use Candlestick charts and replace them with a line and take the turning and standard lines off your chart altogether. You will lose some additional information, but this might be a price worth paying for the increased clarity. It is important to get your charts set to a level which is best for you to be able to read them.

Chart 8-16: Chart of Dow Jones Index configured with price as line chart

## Summary points

- Turning Line - midpoint of the high and low of the last 9 sessions
- Standard Line - midpoint of the high and low of the last 26 sessions
- Cloud Span A - midpoint of turning line and standard line shifted 26 bars forward
- Cloud Span B - midpoint of high and low of last 52 sessions shifted 26 bars forward
- The Lagging Line - the price line (close) shifted back 26 bars
- Configure your Cloud Charts in a way that they are clearest to you

# Chapter 9 - **Interpreting Cloud Charts**

The most important aspect with Cloud Charts is how the price interacts with the cloud. Time and time again you will see prices turn right on the edge of the cloud. The price effectively creates 'a rod for its own back' into the future with the cloud mechanism. It interacts with the cloud running ahead of itself on a perpetual basis providing us with a unique roadmap. Below we see how Antofagasta made a number of points of contact with the cloud in 2009.

Chart 9-1: Price making contact with the cloud

Cloud touches aren't always precise, but prices often make contact and rebound or run along the cloud edges as we see below with Aviva shares. Prices can interact with outer and inner edges of the cloud.

Chart 9-2: Price testing the cloud base for Aviva, support

The chart below shows touches of the cloud from below with the British Pound against the Dollar. Cloud Charts work especially well for currencies as we will come to see.

Chart 9-3: The British Pound, price testing the cloud from either side

## Bullish and bearish zones

One of the biggest advantages of Cloud Charts is that we can know immediately if the picture is bullish or bearish. As with Point and Figure charts this is completely objective. If the price is above the cloud it is bullish, we are in an uptrend and prices are going up. If the price is below the cloud it is bearish, we are in a downtrend with prices continuing to fall. You can run through hundreds of charts in minutes knowing whether each one is bullish or bearish in a second. Try it!

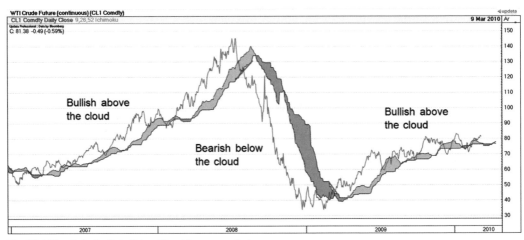

Chart 9-4: The oil chart with bullish and bearish zones marked

There is an exception to prices being above or below the cloud and that is when they are actually buried in the cloud itself. Resolving this is quite simple. It is the direction that you entered the cloud that counts. If prices came into the cloud from above (this will normally be a blue cloud) the picture is still bullish. If they came into the cloud from below (red cloud) this is still bearish territory. But this state is also the crunch point. Will the cloud provide support (uptrend) or resistance (downtrend) here? Or will the line cross the cloud thereby making a transition from one state to the other? When prices are in the cloud you should be at a state of heightened alert due to this increased uncertainty.

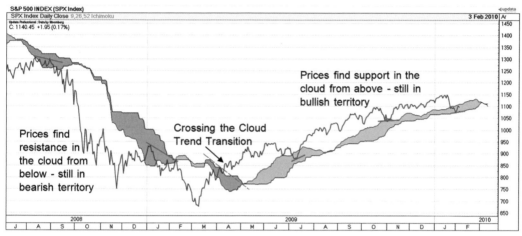

Chart 9-5: Anatomy of price action with the cloud

In fact the crossing barrier is the slower span B (52 bar midpoint shifted 26 bars forward) highlighted here along the edge of cloud. You can thicken this on your charts to highlight the boundary for the price.

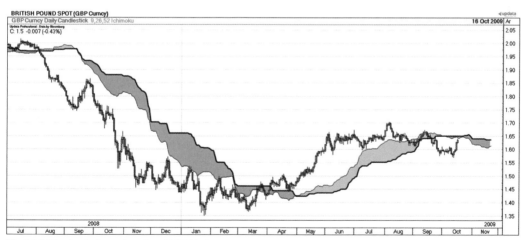

Chart 9-6: The cloud edge, or boundary, highlighted

You can simplify this even further by looking at how the price line (blue) interacts with cloud span B (black) as shown below. But concealing the cloud gives up information about other areas of support and resistance which we will come to see.

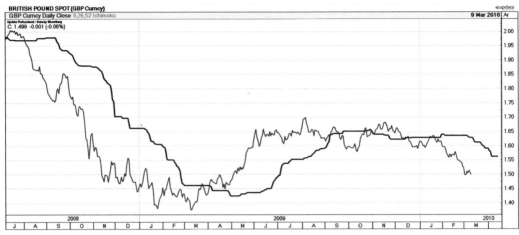

Chart 9-7: The price line and Cloud Span B

While cloud thickness is not regarded as a signal in itself, it is worth noting that clouds become thickest when prices are accelerating in the trend direction shorter term. Span A is moving quickly and further away from Span B. There comes a point where this divergence is not sustainable and prices will enter a consolidation with the trend or undergo a reversal. When the cloud spans cross, the cloud changes direction and prices will cross the cloud if the new trend is sustained. We will look at this further Part 3, but if the cloud starts to become thinner from an unusually fat state, that is a sign that the trend could change with prices crossing the cloud. The cloud is often thicker at the turning points as shown below.

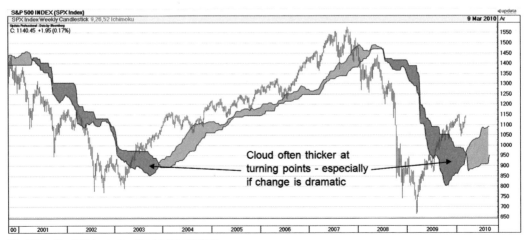

Chart 9-8: Cloud thickness can signal a top or bottom

So, let's conduct our first Cloud Chart analysis of the chart below.

1. The price is above the cloud which is bullish
2. The cloud is blue at the end of the chart. The cloud colour at the extreme right is usually something we notice at an instant indicating bullishness or bearishness
3. The price tested the cloud base in July 2009 and the cloud top in October 2009. This historical interaction tells us the cloud is providing clear support in this uptrend.
4. The turning line is above the standard line telling us that the shorter term picture is bullish

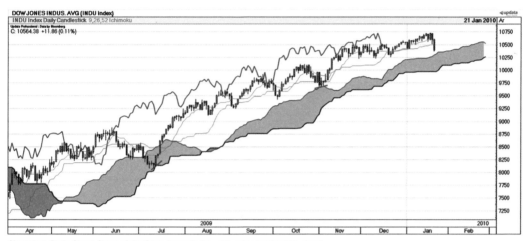

Chart 9-9: Daily Cloud Chart of the Dow Jones Index with price testing the cloud

Overall this cloud chart tells us that we are in an uptrend with no sign of a reversal.

## Main signals

Of course not all Cloud Charts will read this simply and we will study the signals in order of importance. Some experienced cloud chart technicians may rank these and other signals differently, but if you are new to the subject this order is recommended.

1. Lagging line crossing the cloud
2. Price crossing the cloud (will nearly always occur before a lagging line cross)
3. Price and lagging line touching the cloud
4. The cloud spans crossing (the cloud changes colour far right of chart)
5. The turning line crossing the standard line

## Lagging line crossing the cloud

The lagging line will nearly always cross the cloud after the price has and it is the true confirming signal that the trend has changed. When this happens, especially after a long clear trend beforehand, the price will already be clearly in the new counter trend territory. Lagging line signals occur later than signals given by the price alone crossing the cloud, but failed signals are much less common.

Here we see the lagging line cross the cloud. Notice the point where the price was when this cross occurred. It is important to appreciate that this occurs at a later date on the chart's x-axis because of the 26 bar offset. So in this case the lagging line cross did not occur until mid December, when the price was at $1.44.

Chart 9-10: Price and the Lagging Line crossing the cloud

The lagging line will frequently interact with the cloud. Here we see an example of the lagging line testing the cloud base for support in November and then finding resistance on the top of the cloud before making the cloud cross. This tight interaction with the cloud boundaries, given the length of the previous uptrend, also lends weight to the significance of the cloud cross and we can see a new downtrend is starting.

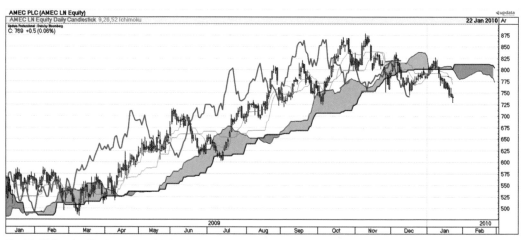

Chart 9-11: Lagging Line interaction with the cloud

Here we see it again with Marks and Spencer plc. You will find numerous examples of the lagging line doing this price whipsaw in the cloud if you scroll through charts of stocks.

Chart 9-12: Lagging line 'whipsaw' in the cloud

## Price crossing the cloud

The price crossing the cloud is a signal that can be traded on, but there is a greater risk of a failed signal than with a lagging line cross. It may suit some traders to take the earlier signal and exit if it transpires to be a false cross. It will come down to trading style and is another example of the risk reward conundrum that traders and investors face. Price interaction with the cloud does tend to be less clear cut than the lagging line cross as we see in the chart above. The price will often seesaw about the cloud crossing a few times before the trend change occurs. So as well as a lower likelihood of a false signal, the lagging line crosses are easier to read during a trend transition. There is another answer to whether you should use price as your signal or the lagging line which falls with in line with a general rule in technical analysis. Use the method that has been giving the clearer signals historically.

Below we see an example where the lagging line has given one clear transition for gold while the price has crossed the cloud several times during the recent uptrend. As a result, you would use the lagging line for reading a trend cross over a price cross.

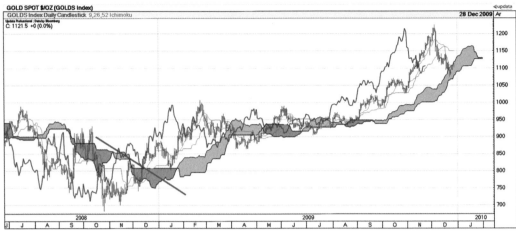

Chart 9-13: Cloud transition for Gold

On the other hand, the Dow Jones chart below shows that the price has not crossed the cloud any more frequently than the one lagging line cross in the past couple of years. In this case you might attach more importance to a cloud cross. It is worth noting the cost of the later signal here. The Dow crossed the cloud in April at 7750 points. By the time the lagging line had crossed a month later (where the price is on the x-axis) the Dow was at 8250 points.

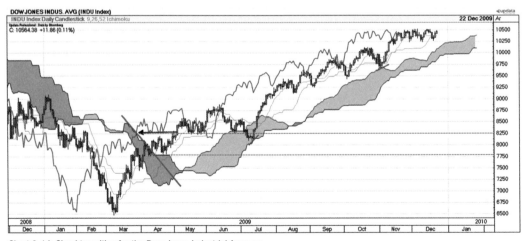

Chart 9-14: Cloud transition for the Dow Jones Industrial Average

Candlestick chart signals can lend extra value when reading Cloud Charts too. For instance here we see the lagging line crossed above the cloud for the Japanese stock market. Referring to the price at this point we see an island reversal pattern was occurring. In fact we don't know the reversal has occurred until the end of the day following the 'marooned' reversal candle. As with many candle patterns, you need all three candles to see the pattern is completed. So if the price has gapped up, as we see here, and the lagging line has crossed the cloud, it may be worth waiting one extra day to avoid a false signal.

Chart 9-15: Island Reversal as a temporary cloud breach for the Nikkei 225 Index

Whether the cloud cross is read using the price or lagging line, the idea that either of them test the cloud from both sides is an important part of confirming a trend change has occurred. The idea that resistance becomes support and vice versa is well recognised in traditional technical analysis techniques. If you see it before and after the cloud cross you can be much more certain that you have a trend change in progress. Here we see several touches either side of the cloud with the New Zealand Dollar.

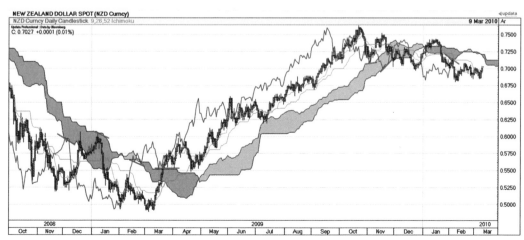

Chart 9-16: New Zealand Dollar testing the cloud from either side

## Thinking time from the cloud

The fact that the cloud is projected forward 26 sessions into the future is really valuable for any trader. One of the biggest complaints in missing opportunities is that things happened so quickly that it was too late to do anything. The cloud projected forward gives you a 'thinking time' advantage whereby you are more prepared and ready to do something when the picture starts to change. This is synonymous to what we are taught when learning to drive a car. We learn that the distance travelled, from the instant we see we need to brake, to the moment we put our foot on the brake, is greater than the distance from braking to stopping. Cloud Charts give you a feel about the price going forward and this subliminal element is what makes them so appealing.

The forward projection of the cloud also gives you a feel of what the price needs to do going forward in order to stay in a trend. Take this chart of oil below. If the price closes below $74.75 at any time in the next 40 days, this will cause the lagging line to move below the cloud. We have our first move below the uptrend in months. But this level doesn't stay constant into the future. We have a map of what the price needs to do after that as time progresses. For the first two weeks in February on this chart the burden of trend support starts to increase for the price until around the middle of that month it is at $75.25 going forward. This will change as the price changes. The price creates a future burden for itself with the cloud mechanism as time elapses. The lagging line has the same burden but a further 26 sessions on. So from this chart we can say that if the oil price is below $75.25 in mid March, the lagging line will have crossed into bearish territory.

Chart 9-17: The cloud setting forward requirements for price on Oil

## Cloud spans crossing

Sometimes the most immediately visible sign of a trend change may simply be the cloud spans crossing at the extreme right of a chart. This tends to be because most clouds are colour coded based on the relative positions of the spans. This is not a widely used signal and you should wait for a proper transition, but if the cloud is changing like this, it is worth noting.

On the next chart we see Procter & Gamble shares with such a cloud change at the end of the chart. It is also worth noting here that we had a couple of cloud span crosses before that didn't lead to anything. A degree of judgement will need to be used to assess whether the spans crossing are more significant than previous temporary crosses.

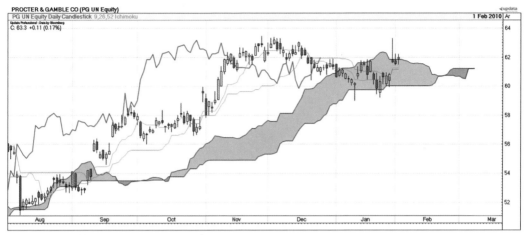

Chart 9-18: Cloud Spans showing a possible temporary cross

## Turning line crossing the standard line

As we have identified, these lines can be read like moving averages and they give shorter term signals with more frequent crosses than the signals covered so far. Some Ichimoku chartists see them as very important while others might take them off their charts altogether. There are some instances where these crosses are useful. One trading strategy is to trade with the trend and take the cross with that trend for an entry and the counter trend cross for an exit. So, in an uptrend you would buy on the turning line crossing up through the standard line and sell when it crosses below. In a downtrend trade short, by selling on the turning line crossing below the standard line and exit the short trade when it crosses back above it.

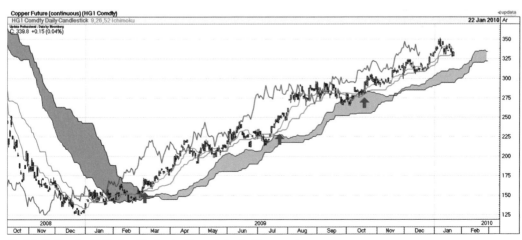

Chart 9-19: Signals with the trend for turning line and standard line crossing

When the price has moved along way from the chart, a useful counter trend signal is the turning line crossing the standard line. Here we see an example where gold prices ran a long way from the cloud and the first signal from the extreme was the cross of these lines as shown.

Chart 9-20: Turning line and standard line crossing when a long way from the cloud

The same applies in reverse: if prices fall a long way below a cloud in bearish territory, the turning line crossing up through the standard line might present a buying opportunity. In each case there is a risk that you are trading against the prevailing trend, this might be fine for closing a profitable position in the absence of other signals, but entering a trade counter trend can be risky. There are other ways to resolve the price moving a long way from the cloud which we will cover in the next chapter.

In addition to using the turning line and standard line as you would use two moving averages, each line can be used in the same way as you would use only one average with the price. The price will often cross the turning line too frequently for it to be of any great benefit, but the slower standard line can interact with the price. As with the 26 day moving average with the price for touches or support and resistance as well as crosses, the standard line can be used. On the next chart we see how shares in American Express found support on the standard line for the last few months in 2009. The cross could be taken more seriously in January as a result. The cloud did provide support after crossing the standard line, as we would expect, but you may have been keen to sell nearer the highs for the month.

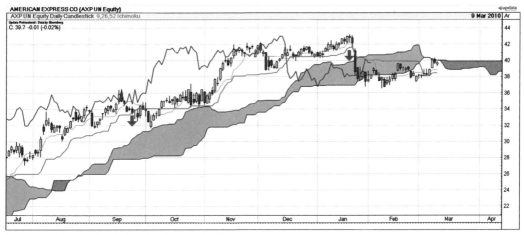

Chart 9-21: Price crossing the Standard line as a signal

## Using clouds as your trading roadmap

Perhaps the most valuable aspect of Cloud Charts is the objective definition of trend state that you get at a glance. You know immediately whether you are in a bullish (uptrend) or a bearish (downtrend) trend so you can adjust your stance accordingly. It may well be that you don't use the trading signals discussed in this chapter and rely on other techniques. But the cloud will always tell you whether you should be taking long trades in an uptrend or short trades in a downtrend.

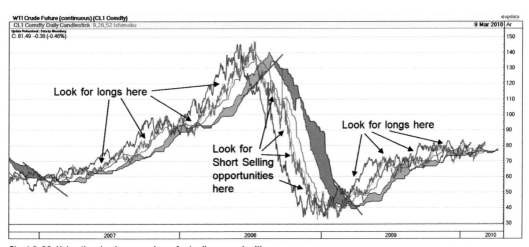

Chart 9-22: Using the cloud as a roadmap for trading opportunities

## Congestion and sideways markets

Because Cloud Charts are a trend following technique, due to the mechanism of shifting the cloud forward they generally do not work well in a long consolidation phase of prices running sideways. You will find this frequently. If the price is going sideways as shown on the chart of the British Pound below, then you have to accept that the chart will be difficult to interpret. The price, lagging line and cloud will simply be superimposing themselves over one another, making the chart difficult to read. There is little you can do with a chart like this other than wait for prices to start moving away from the cloud as they did in August 2009 here. Remember that these sorts of sideways patterns are more often a continuation pattern than a reversal. There are ways to trade these zones with shorter term charts which we will look at in the next chapter.

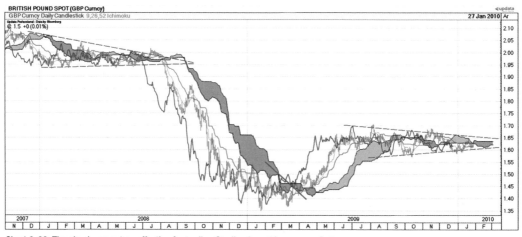

Chart 9-23: The cloud was not as effective for trading Sterling in a sideways market

## Altering the cloud chart construction periods

Cloud Charts use 9, 26 and 52 as the standard construction periods. These periods do seem to work best across the full range of financial instruments in back-tests. We will look at back-testing in Part 3 and how the cloud construction periods can be optimised. You will nearly always be able to prove that one set of periods worked better for a given instrument than the standard 9, 26 and 52 periods. Whether that set of optimised periods will work better going forward will be harder to prove. And whether there is a better set to use across all asset classes would be harder to show still. You may change the periods and on the next page we see a chart below using 8, 21 and 55 (Fibonacci numbers) as the periods. However, unless you are extremely proficient with optimisation and regularly running thorough back-tests, it is recommended you stick with the standard 9, 26 and 52 periods as your default Cloud Chart.

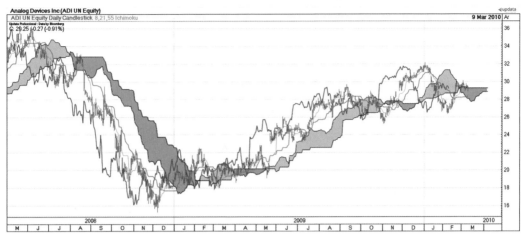

Chart 9-24: Cloud Chart with different construction periods

## Why do Cloud Charts work?

Students of the subject often ask why the 9, 26 and 52 periods work best. It is not easy to say why but we do know from the history that Hosoda and his team spent years in the 1930s arriving at these periods, a sort of human back-test before the age of computers. People often point out that the charts must be self fulfilling with everybody using the same periods and getting the same signals. This may be the case for certain instruments in Japan, where Clouds Charts are heavily used, but there is still a lot of room for subjective interpretation. Lots of market participants using them will see different things at different times and will behave quite differently in the way they trade the market.

Why does the technique itself actually work? Again this is hard to prove, but a growing number of people are using it and this looks set to increase dramatically if the rate of adoption in dealing rooms in recent years is anything to go by. Perhaps the simplest reason of all why Cloud Charts seem to work goes back to the diagram we drew on page 30, where we identified that you could only truly know a top or a bottom retrospectively. The construction mechanism that shifts the cloud forward and the lagging line back leads to a situation where we get crossover points after a high or a low. Seeing such a trend change from the price line itself is much harder as we are left trying to imagine when the change happened. Cloud Charts will also often define a new trend much earlier than when it becomes visually clear using trend lines. This early trend definition is another advantage that the cloud provides.

Emotionally, we have the knowledge that the top and bottom occurred, and feel we have missed the opportunity to act. The cloud presents the chart differently showing us the real event is the trend change, not the high or low that we had little or no chance of knowing. The combination of the 9, 26, and 52 session construction periods is the added ingredient that seems to make these charts work consistently well when the trend has changed. Most of all Cloud Charts are the ultimate hard coded tool for ensuring you make the trend your friend.

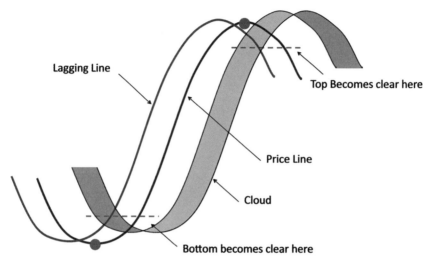

Figure 9-1: Why Cloud Charts work

## Summary points

- Prices above the cloud means a bullish picture
- Prices below the cloud means a bearish picture
- Prices in the cloud are bullish if they came from the bullish zone
- Prices in the cloud are bearish if they came from the bearish zone
- Historically thick clouds after a run in prices might signal an imminent trend change
- The lagging line crossing the cloud is the main signal of a trend change
- Price crossing the cloud is an earlier but less reliable warning of a trend change
- Prices and the lagging line will often find support or resistance on the cloud edges
- The cloud spans crossing may be a sign that the trend is changing
- The turning line crossing the lagging line a long way from the cloud is a potential signal
- Cloud Charts don't work particularly well in sideways price congestion zones
- You may change the construction periods, but it is not recommended
- Cloud Charts will normally define a new trend earlier than it becomes clear using trend lines

# Chapter 10 - **Multiple Time Frame Analysis**

So far all of the charts we have looked at have been daily charts. One of the most powerful aspects of technical analysis is that all the principles we have applied so far to daily charts can be used in the same manner on charts of other time frames. This is especially true of Cloud Charts.

## Time Horizon

Simply by changing the frame of your chart you are changing your time horizon.
The screen below shows six charts of the same instrument with the same period moving averages. Moving from the top left chart clockwise, we have a monthly, a weekly, a daily, an hourly, a ten minute chart and a one minute chart. The Candlesticks in these charts are constructed from the open, high, low, close prices for those periods. The averages are 21 month, 21 week, 21, day, 21 hour, 21 ten minute and 21 minute averages respectively.
All the tools are read in the same way but your time horizon is now governed in each case according to the time frame of the chart.

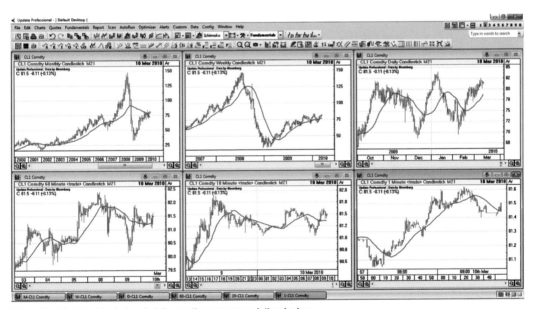

Figure 10-1: Technical Analysis principles are the same on each time horizon

The chart below is a weekly Candlestick chart of copper with a 14 week moving average and 21 week RSI, with 21 week moving average of the RSI. This would be viewed and analysed in the same way as with a daily chart, but by removing the daily noise you have a clearer longer term picture.

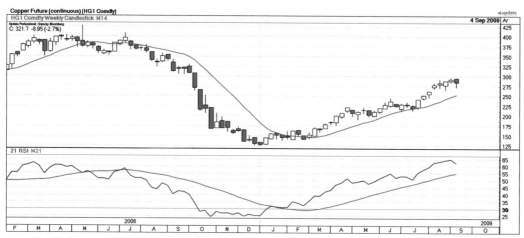

Chart 10-1: Weekly chart analysed in the same way as a daily chart

Similarly, the 60 minute Candlestick chart of the Australian dollar below, shows up information that you would never see in the daily or weekly charts.

Chart 10-2: 60 minute chart for Australian Dollar with MACD and MACD Histogram

Getting your time horizon right is one of the most important aspects of technical analysis. You need to make sure you are looking at the correct time frame chart to match your time horizon. Using multiple time frames with Cloud Charts adds an extra dimension to trading.

## What's your time horizon?

If you are ever asked for a view on a particular instrument, the first question you should be asking back before you give an opinion is "What's your time horizon?" Until you know this, it is impossible to give an educated reply to the question. At the very least you should define the time horizon of your view before answering. The chart of gold below highlights this problem. Is it in an uptrend or a downtrend? It will depend on which trend you are looking at.

Chart 10-3: Chart of Gold. What is the current trend?

Referring back to Dow Theory covered in Chapter 2 we can probably answer the question on this daily chart alone. But looking at the weekly chart we see the answer is more clear cut.

Chart 10-4: Weekly chart for gold with clearer trend

## Time frame selection

Knowing which time frame chart to select for your time horizon takes experience, and this is an area of trading and investing that is not well documented for newcomers. A big part of the problem is that people have different definitions of what short term and long term time horizons are. A fund manager focused on quarterly performance with a 'buy and hold' strategy, might define short term as a few weeks. A currency trader might consider a few weeks to be very long term. This creates a dilemma in defining time horizon right away. The almost infinite range of time horizons with millions of market participants makes financial markets even more complex.

The table below sets out to address two main problems. The first is to define what short, medium and long term actually means for the market as a whole. If you are a longer term trader or a shorter term investor you will gravitate towards the middle of the table and find the definitions acceptable. Long term investors and short term traders may struggle with the left and right hand ends of the table respectively and may prefer the definitions at the bottom. The setting of the definition is most valuable when dealing with other traders and investors and it is always a good idea to define your time horizons first – i.e. Medium term = weeks.

Whichever adjectives you use to define your time horizon, it is the nouns that will truly count in setting the time frame chart you should select. This is the second problem that the simple table below sets out to solve and it is really easy to remember because the time horizon is one step ahead of the chart frame. For instance, if you are thinking weeks ahead - use daily charts, days ahead – use hourly, or months ahead – use weekly. Just remember daily charts are not about understanding price movement in the next few days. The same will apply to other time frames.

| | ULTRA SHORT | VERY SHORT | SHORT TERM | MEDIUM TERM | LONG TERM | VERY LONG | ULTRA LONG |
|---|---|---|---|---|---|---|---|
| Time Horizon | Minutes | Hours | Days | Weeks | Months | Years | Many Years |
| Chart Frame | tick/1 Min | 5/10 Mins | Hourly | Daily | Weekly | Monthly | Quarterly |
| Cloud Extends | 30 Mins | 2-4 Hours | 3 Days | 1 Month | 6 Months | 2 Years | 8 Years |

| SHORT TERM TRADER | | | LONG TERM INVESTOR | | |
|---|---|---|---|---|---|
| SHORT | MEDIUM | LONG | SHORT | MEDIUM | LONG |

Figure 10-2: Linton's Trading Time Horizon Table

## Cloud Charts and Time Horizon

No other chart deals with time horizons more simply than Cloud Charts. The first reason for this is that the cloud extends forward 26 bars, forcing you visually to think ahead. The table above includes the rough time that the cloud extends forward for each time frame chart. The cloud makes you think the appropriate distance ahead for whatever chart frame you are using. For example, if you are thinking about where the oil price will be in 6 months time you should use the weekly chart as shown on the next page.

Chart 10-5: Weekly cloud chart for oil

The second reason why Cloud Charts deal with time frames so well is that switching the time frame is the only thing you need to do to change the time horizon of your analysis. No other technique allows you to switch your time frame and get a new clear picture like Cloud Charts do. Point and Figure Charts come close by allowing you to set your box size – medium term 1% of price, long term 2%, short term 0.5%, but the speed at which you can get the full picture with the clouds is invaluable. The screen below shows the same picture we saw on page 147 but now with Cloud Charts. Before we even do any individual analysis on the charts we can say – monthly = bullish, weekly = bearish, daily = bullish, hourly = bearish, 10 minute = bearish, 1 minute = bullish.

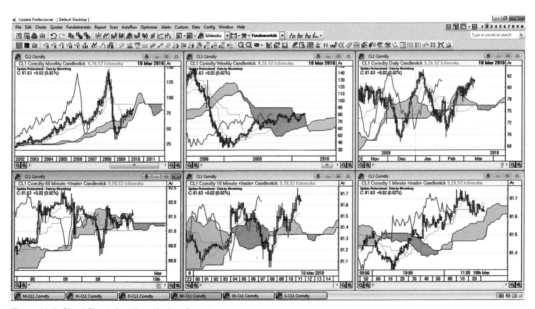

Figure 10-3: Cloud Charts for oil on six time frames

## Multiple time frame analysis example

So let's look at each of the six charts in more detail and carry out a multiple time frame Cloud Chart analysis highlighting the salient points as we go.

### Very long term – Several years – Monthly - Bullish

The price and the lagging line are above the cloud, so the picture is bullish. Notice how the lagging line bounced right on the top of the cloud (marked) confirming support and the cloud has been lending support to the price in recent months at the edge of the cloud. Support for the price is $65 but given the previous breach we would pay more attention to the lagging line support level at around $50 next year. If the price does keep running up the cloud, we will be back above $100 a year or two out.

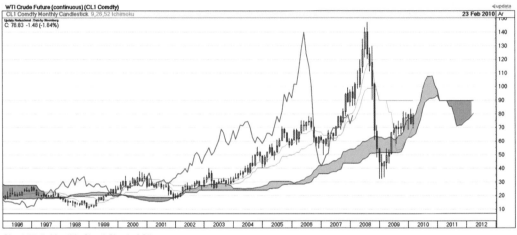

Chart 10-6: Monthly Cloud Chart of Oil

### Long term – Several months – Weekly - Bearish

The top chart on the next page shows the price and the lagging line are below the cloud which is bearish. The price has just confirmed resistance at the cloud as marked. The cloud at the end of the chart is blue in line with the monthly chart's bullish state. We have price resistance at around $81 and the lagging line would need to get through $90 for the picture to become bullish. If prices can break $90 we would expect this to be a floor for the price for some time. We would watch for it holding at this level.

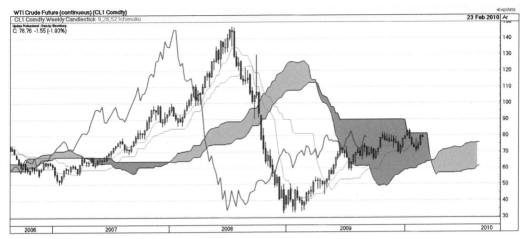

Chart 10-7: Weekly Cloud Chart of Oil

## Medium term – Several weeks - Daily - Bullish

The daily chart has been our medium term roadmap for the oil price. It has given excellent signals for the trend changing in recent years so we have come to trust this chart's ability to tell us the trading environment we are in. The price has breached the cloud and it may well do again, but it is the lagging line that is key. While it is above the cloud we are bullish. The price would need to close below the $73.50 level for at least a day or two, to be safe, before we could conclude the uptrend was over. An intra-day breach would not be enough. The turning line has cut down through the standard line which is an Ichimoku sell signal but it is late and counter trend. The price is testing support now and both it and the lagging line would give sell signals in this case with a close below $73.

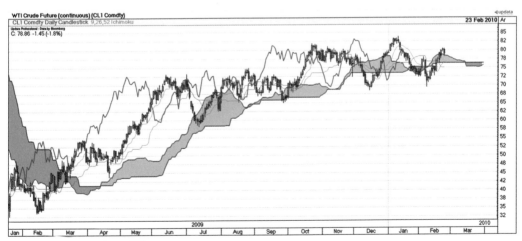

Chart 10-8: Daily Cloud Chart of Oil

## Short term – Several days – Hourly – Bullish

The 60 minute chart has also been an excellent road map for identifying the short term trend in recent months and is now bullish above the cloud.

Chart 10-9: 60 minute Cloud Chart of Oil

## Very short term – Several hours – 10 minute bars – Bearish

The ten minute chart is in bearish territory for the current trading day.

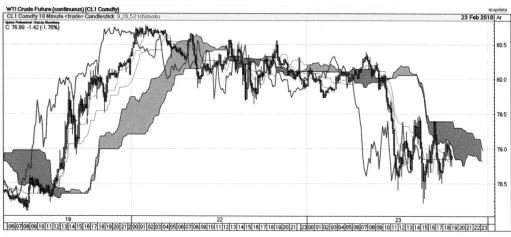

Chart 10-10: 10 minute Cloud Chart of Oil

## Ultra short term – Half an hour – 1 minute – Bullish

Here in the last couple of hours, the minute chart has turned bullish.

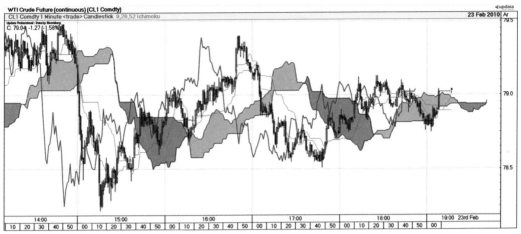

Chart 10-11: 1 minute Cloud Chart of Oil

You can see that Cloud Charts give you a multi-faceted view of the market very quickly. You can do this with other technical analysis techniques, but none of them allows you to move through the analysis so quickly with a very clear view of each time frame. It is the powerful 'one look' advantage of Ichimoku that makes this possible.

It is always worth summarising your analysis and keeping it in front of you so that you can clearly resolve all the time frame views at once. You might do this on one of your computer screens, with multiple charts open or print out several charts on a page and pin it up in front of you as a reminder. You might produce a matrix like the one below and colour code it. When prices look set to cross the cloud you may set your view to neutral and colour code it accordingly.

| Very Long Term | Several Years | Monthly | Bullish |
| Long Term | Several Months | Weekly | Bearish |
| Medium Term | Several Weeks | Daily | Bullish |
| Short Term | Several Days | Hourly | Bearish |
| Very Short Term | Several Hours | 10 mins | Bearish |

If you are in the business of advising clients, this sort of time frame view can help avoid the confusion that can arise when giving a view. It is not enough to say you are bullish or bearish, unless all time frames point that way. It is rare for several time frames to all be pointing the same way. Prices moving in trends within trends within trends means, that they will be on different parts of each cycle.

It is best to reference your view with your time horizon first such as; 'by medium term, with daily charts looking out several weeks,' and then state your view, 'we are bullish.' And then, "The very long term in the years ahead looks bullish, but the picture less long term, several months out, does currently look bearish. Prices should perform well in the weeks ahead but might struggle for a few months after that."

## Moving up or down a frame

As a general rule you should always look up and down a time frame from your preferred time horizon when using Cloud Charts. This means that you should be watching three charts, preferably simultaneously. Obviously the picture on the shortest term time frame, of your chosen three, will change more quickly. You will not have to refer to your longest term time frame as much. Sometimes four or five time frames can give you more of a picture, but generally three around your central time frame will be enough. Having this view either side will keep you abreast of the extremes of your view that may not show up on your preferred chart.

One of the most likely times you will need to look at adjacent time frames are when prices have moved a long way from the cloud so that you have no idea of where support or resistance is. The next longer time frame might provide you with ideas of resistance and support, especially if prices are retracing in the bigger picture. Here we see Boeing making new highs on the daily chart.

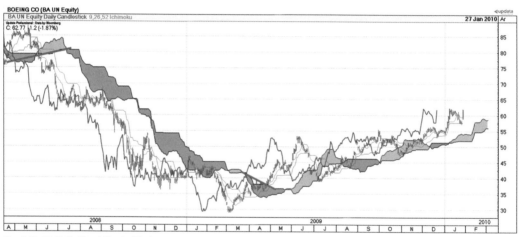

Chart 10-12: Daily Cloud Chart of Boeing

If we look to the weekly chart we see the lagging line hitting cloud resistance. The chart may be breached, but if you are about to buy the shares you may want to wait and see. As a general rule, counter trend rallies require you to look at the longer term chart for where a rally should run out of steam.

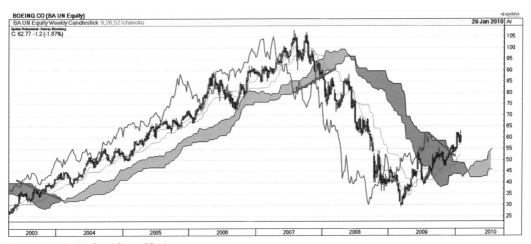

Chart 10-13: Weekly Cloud Chart of Boeing

When prices have moved a long way from the cloud and are starting to turn, you should look to the shorter term time frame to see if you have a cloud cross signal. Here we see the gold chart in 2009 which was making new all time highs, which will mean the longer term time frames will not have any clouds above the price. As prices got so far from the cloud, you might decide to look to an hourly chart which would show a turning point first.

Chart 10-14: Daily Cloud Chart of Gold

The chart below is the 60 minute chart for gold which shows the recent cloud cross to bearish territory.

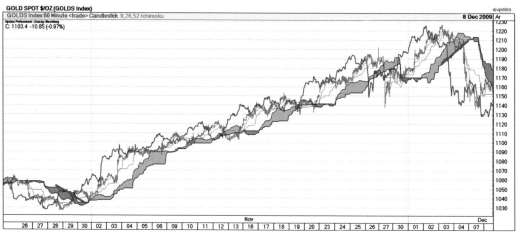

Chart 10-15: 60 minute Cloud Chart of Gold

The other time you may choose to turn to a Cloud Chart of a different time frame is when the price action has become congested. Because Cloud Charts are trend following, they do not work well when prices are range bound as we see with the daily chart of the British Pound against the US Dollar below.

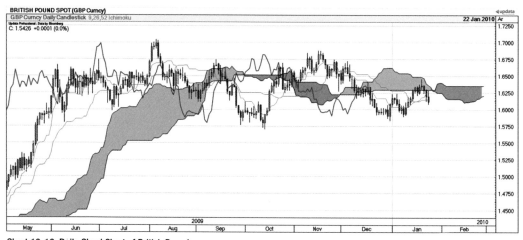

Chart 10-16: Daily Cloud Chart of British Pound

Move to the longer term weekly chart and the reason for the congestion at cloud resistance becomes crystal clear.

Chart 10-17: Weekly Cloud Chart of British Pound

Similarly, if you wish to trade this range, the daily chart will be of little use and you will need to drop to a shorter term time frame to see if it provides better signals. Here we see the hourly chart of Sterling.

Chart 10-18: 60 minute Cloud Chart of British Pound

## Finding a short term time frame that works best

It is sometimes the case with the intraday charts that the standard 5, 10 or 60 minute charts don't work so well. When this happens you may need to explore other time frames such as 15, 20 or 30 minute charts. Some traders use 240 minute charts for their clouds. You could even consider the Fibonacci numbers as your time frame. The key thing is that the charts have been visually easy to read with clear movement either side of the cloud and decisive crossing signals. The chart below is a 15 minute chart for Oil which seems to have worked better than 5 or 10 minutes in the time shown.

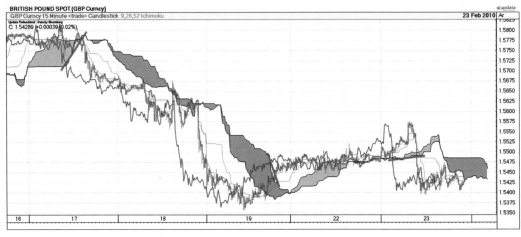

Chart 10-19: 15 minute Cloud Chart of British Pound

## Multiple time frame analysis limitations

It may not always be possible to analyse multiple time frames. For instance monthly numbers such as inflation or house prices will mean you are limited to quarterly and yearly time frames. While the monthly data will force you to think years ahead, the yearly data (if you have enough) will be looking out decades. Liquidity or certain instruments or small company shares might also be an issue, such that intra-day trades barely occur. All technical analysis techniques will face a similar disadvantage and if you don't have the time series data to construct the Cloud Charts, then you won't be able to analyse them.

## Summary points

- Cloud Charts work in the same way on any time frame chart
- The time frame of the chart governs your Time horizon
- Always look at more than one Cloud Chart time frame on any instrument
- Define your own time horizon definitions with a clear table or matrix
- Start with long term time frames and progress increasingly shorter term
- Record your views and analysis for each time frame

# Chapter 11 - **Japanese Pattern Techniques**

In Chapter 1 we looked at the history of Cloud Charts. Hosoda, who first developed the chart, did not make great reference to the analysis of multiple time frames. This was almost certainly due to the work involved in plotting all the data points manually before the advent of computers. Hidenobu Sasaki's book, written in 1996, does not cover the subject of multiple time frames either. All of the charts in the book are daily charts. Even as recently as the mid 1990s computerised Ichimoku charts were not common. As computers have become more powerful, the ability to switch rapidly between data intensive intra-day time frames has increased. Many traders now have several screens on their desk enabling them to see dozens of different charts simultaneously. The idea of viewing multiple time frames, say weekly, daily, hourly, 10 minute, of the same instrument and analysing them all is something that many traders now do in practice. Multiple time frame analysis of Clouds Charts may have been conducted in the 1990s, but it has not really been documented until now.

Sasaki's book did cover three other areas of Ichimoku analysis under topics he called; wave principle, price target and time span. The vast majority of people using Cloud Charts in the Western world do not use these Japanese principles. We have seen up to now that Cloud Chart analysis is an objective technique with a degree of subjective interpretation. The concepts in this chapter are more subjective ideas which are therefore more difficult to apply. If you choose not to use these additional techniques and to simply apply Cloud Charts as we have learned them so far, you should still find Cloud Chart analysis to be valuable. The multiple time frame approach, seemingly not heavily used historically in Japan, is likely to be quicker and more reliable for newcomers to Cloud Charts.

## Wave Principle

While computers are very good at taking time series data, constructing charts and switching from one time frame to another instantly, they are still less good at dealing with highly subjective techniques such as pattern definition. The first aspect of the wave principle in Ichimoku analysis looks to identify a number of different price patterns. While some of the patterns are recognisable in line with those we covered in Chapter 2, most will be new to Western technicians. Curiously these patterns in Japan are named after letters of the English language alphabet. The patterns apparently resemble the price action they are labelling more closely than Japanese characters. Here we identify the main patterns as Sasaki set them out in his book.

Figure 11-1: Ichimoku pattern elements

The 'I' is just a simple straight line continuous move in prices and not really one that Western technicians would identify as a pattern. The 'V' is what we might call a single top or bottom and would not be as significant as a double top or a double bottom. The 'N' pattern is what we would recognise as a pull back within a trend. The 'P' is like a pennant or symmetrical triangle and the 'Y' is like an ascending triangle. Combinations of the basic letter patterns are also possible with some shown below.

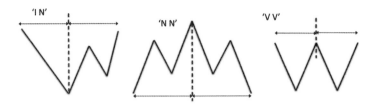

Figure 11-2: Some examples of combined Ichimoku patterns

There is also a variation which is termed a '4' which identifies a 4 wave formation.

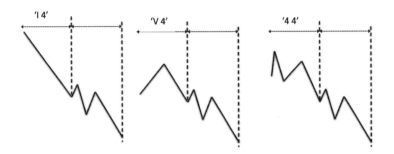

Figure 11-3:

Elliot Wave Theory, a Western technique (only briefly mentioned in Part 1) is broadly based around the idea that prices move in 5 waves in the primary trend and 3 waves in the reactive trend. The chart of the Dax Index below makes identification of the waves easier by isolating the moves greater than 10%.

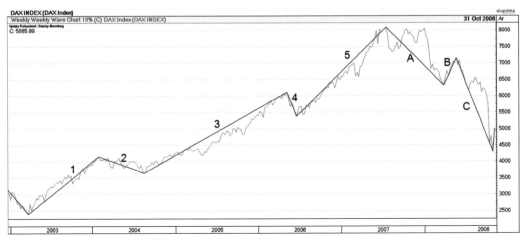

Chart 11-1: 10% wave chart of the DAX Index

There are several more rules to this technique and it is one of the more subjective Western charting methods. Two experienced Ellioticians may easily disagree on which wave is which. The wave principle outlined in Sasaki's book on the Ichimoku technique is even more subjective as it is not constrained by the 5 x 3 wave roadmap and any number of waves may be present. His book suggests that all price movement can be broken into the patterns identified in this chapter. It is true that the 'I' and 'V do give you the flexibility of naming moves in between. The 5% wave chart of the Nikkei 225 Index below has possible patterns labelled.

Chart 11-2: N and V price targets on the Nikkei 225 Index

## Price Targets

The 'V' and 'N' patterns in cloud analysis allow price targets to be determined and perhaps the point of labelling every pattern is to isolate the 'V's and 'N's so that we might generate targets from them. The diagrams below show how the targets work and you may recognise some similarities with the patterns covered in Chapter 2. There we identified that the height of the pattern determined the likely extent of the resulting move. The 'V' target below matches this idea. In Chapter 4 we looked at projecting Fibonacci targets (Extensions) from a reactive move after a measured move in prices. We also looked at Point and Figure targets where the target was three times the resultant thrust from a low. The 'N' target below might match these ideas approximately in numerous cases. The targets in this section are probably harder to use than those from the patterns identified in Part 1. Using Point and Figure targets, which is purely rules based, with your Cloud Chart analysis is likely to be more valuable, as we will see in the next chapter.

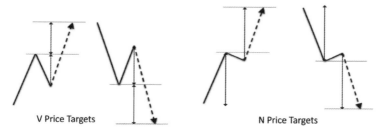

Figure 11-4: V and N Pattern Price Targets

## Time Span Principle

Sasaki's book on Ichimoku charts also covers the idea of projecting when a low or a high will occur at a future date. He uses the key Ichimoku construction numbers of 9 and 26 as well as the midpoint of the two, 17 as the half way point (rounded down from 17.5). The value of 17 approximates 2 x 9 and 26 is almost 3 x 9. The Japanese theory then derives further numbers 33 (near 26 +9), 42 (near 26 + 17), 65 (near 2 x 33), 76 (near 26 x 3), 129 (near 65 x2), with 172 and 257 derived from further variations. Sasaki sets out these numbers early on in his book and then uses them for his time projections.

Not only can price levels be projected with Fibonacci, as shown in Part 1, but future dates for highs or lows can also be projected. The cycle analysis we conducted in Chapter 3 worked on the basis of equidistant cycles, but the time length (period) of price cycles can easily vary. The chart below shows Fibonacci time cycles where each successive cycle point is increased by the golden ratio of 1.618. The idea is that price lows or highs will get further and further apart as time goes on. The days between them will be proportionally in line with 8, 13, 21, 34, 55 etc. The chart below shows how the Fibonacci time projections look. As with price projection targets, the actual cycle lows (or highs) will only fall approximately in line with the projected time the will occur. Some cycles will fit beautifully, others won't at all.

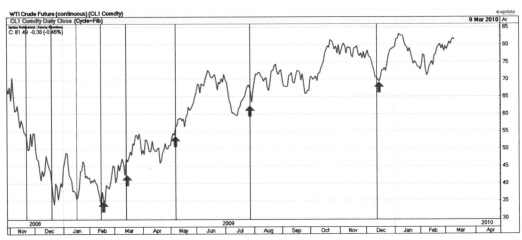

Chart 11-3: Fibonacci cycles for Oil

The time span principle with Cloud Charts looks to achieve something similar to Fibonacci time projections in predicting when prices will make new highs or lows. Knowing the likely time of a turning point in advance can be valuable for when you get there.

At this point it is worth comparing the sequences:

8, 13, 21, 34, 55, 89, 144, 233

9, 17, 26, 33, 42, 65, 76, 129, 172, 257

Only two numbers (8 and 9, 33 and 34) are close and while you are unlikely to use the 257 period often, it is close to the number of trading days in a year. Unlike the Fibonacci number sequence, there is no consistent precise relationship between the adjacent Ichimoku time span numbers.

Sasaki also documented a time span called 'Kihon Suchi' early on in his book, which literally translated means 'basis element' or 'fundamental element.' A simple diagram of this pattern is shown below with the time projections marked.

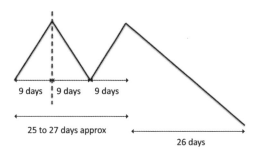

Kihon Suchi Pattern

Figure 11-5: Kihon Suchi Time Target from N wave pattern

Here we see a possible example of the pattern on Japanese Yen. Conducting searches for Kihon Suchi patterns produces very few results which suggests the pattern is quite rare.

Chart 11-4: Kihon Suchi pattern on Japanese Yen

## Price and time projection with Cloud Charts

The Japanese pattern techniques for projecting prices and time are so subjective that it is unlikely that you will use them. For price patterns the Western techniques highlighted in Chapter 2 are easier to learn and likely to serve you better. For targets, the objective rules based technique of Point and Figure is hard to beat. Cloud Charts also have a price and time projection capability built into them by virtue of the cloud running ahead of the price. We know that the cloud span B is always 26 bars ahead of where the price is now and we know where that cloud span is in between. Of all the numbers identified in Sasaki's time span principle, 26 is the most important, and certainly the easiest to identify with the cloud.

On this chart of National Grid we see how the cloud base gives us not only one point where the cycle low may be, but at what price level it will be at whenever it occurs. We also have a further price-time road map with the lagging line and where it can hit the cloud.

Chart 11-5: Daily Cloud Chart of National Grid with future support points

And because the price is rallying on the daily cloud in this case, we can look at where the weekly cloud is for a price target. The short term 60 minute chart might give us even shorter term time price-targets.

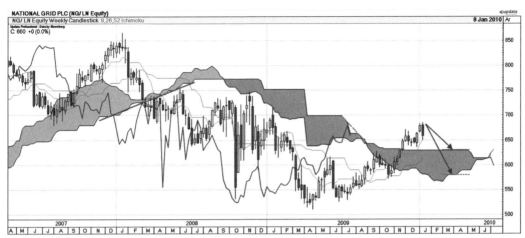

Chart 11-6: Weekly Cloud Chart of National Grid with future support points

This time-price roadmap is one of the most valuable aspects of Cloud Charts and it is not confined to daily and weekly charts. Here we see a monthly chart of the S&P 500 Index which shows how the price needs to be above 1,250 points by the end of 2010 to be in bullish territory again.

Chart 11-7: Using the cloud to identify future cloud levels at given dates

It is also possible to mark the approximate cloud positions of shorter and longer term time frames on a chart. Here we see a daily chart of the Dollar Index with lines where cloud span B are on the weekly and hourly charts.

Chart 11-8: Daily Cloud of Dollar Index with Weekly and 60 minute cloud support marked

The chart below shows a 30 minute chart of the Dollar Index with lines representing cloud span B marked for 5, 10, 30 and 60 minutes.

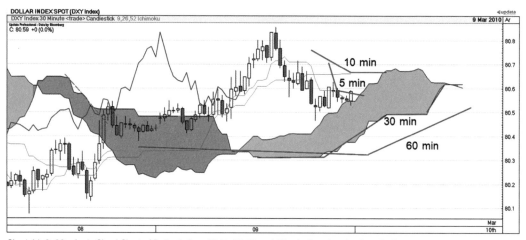

Chart 11-9: 30 minute Cloud Chart of Dollar Index with 5, 10, 30 and 60 minute outer cloud marked

## Summary points

- The Ichimoku wave principle uses the letters I, V, N, P, Y to identify patterns
- Basic price targets may be projected from the V and N patterns
- The time high and low points should occur may be projected
- Cloud Charts already provide price levels at future times with the cloud
- Point and Figure price targets are likely to produce better results

# Chapter 12 - **Cloud Charts with Other Techniques**

In this chapter we will look at bringing the analysis techniques covered in Part 1 together with Cloud Chart analysis. This is done as a practical exercise by looking at the US stock market first and then at a well known US stock.

## US stock market analysis

### Very long term

For the long term picture we start with the monthly Cloud Chart for the S&P 500 Index. From this chart we immediately see that on this time frame, the market is in bearish territory with both price and lagging line below the cloud. There is a resistance level of 1,550 points marked which the market tested twice in early 2000 and late 2007. There is a support level at around 765 points set by the low in 2002 and again in 2009, where prices did briefly go below this level. While the breach is a concern, it is reasonable to say, that over the last thirteen years the market has traded in a wide range between 700 and 1,550 points. Right now prices are in the middle of that range and heading higher.

For the long term picture to be bullish again on the Cloud Chart the price would have to rise above 1,400 points within the next six months. If the S&P 500 Index did jump above 1,200 points in a matter of weeks, we would have the unusual scenario of the lagging line crossing the cloud before the price. The price would need to continue running to more than 1,300 points over the months ahead, without a setback, in order to cross the cloud. If prices move sideways or a little higher over the course of a year, they will be hitting cloud resistance. The price will either struggle at the cloud and fall or break through testing a new 1,100 support level from the other side. The lagging line might take anything up to another two years (26 months behind price) to cross into bullish territory on this chart. Most importantly, we see how the lagging line found strong support on the cloud when the price was making lows in 2002-3 and therefore we should not be surprised to see it testing the cloud from below in the months ahead.

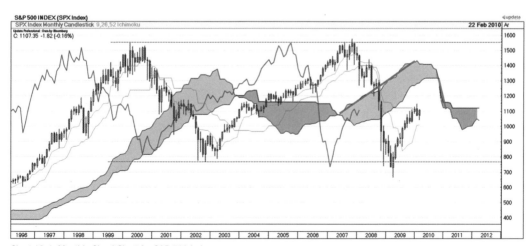

Chart 12-1: Monthly Cloud Chart for S&P 500 Index

The log scale monthly chart below shows the S&P 500 Index over the past twenty years. It might be argued that a large sideways flag pattern is building after a decade which saw the US stock market increase five-fold. If the sideways range we see now is a continuation pattern as part of the very big picture, then when equities do eventually make new all time highs, we could see another very strong decade with prices increasing to a similar extent. The 21 month overbought/oversold indicator shows a cross into positive territory, i.e. the price is now above the 21 month moving average, having been at an historically low oversold level. The 14 and 21 month averages shown on the price chart have not given a golden cross signal yet. The Indexia Market Tracker, a proprietary indicator, has shown a move out of the oversold zone in the last few months and we see how well this indicator stayed in the overbought zone for over a decade, before giving a signal in 2001. The renowned Coppock indicator gave a turn off historically low levels in mid 2009. From this chart we have a number of very long term signals on different indicators.

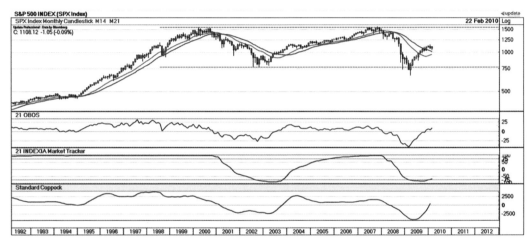

Chart 12-2: Monthly chart for S&P 500 Index with OBOS, INDEXIA Market Tracker and Coppock

The 2% log scale daily Point and Figure Chart at the top of the next page is also a very long term chart, in that a reversal of a least 6% is required to create a change in columns. On this chart the trend is now up and there is an upside target to a new potential all time high. We see the previous price targets have worked well on this chart, having been met or exceeded in each case. The very long term picture, though still bearish on the monthly cloud, is starting to change according to other indicators and tools.

## Long term

The chart at the bottom of the next page shows the longer term picture for the market. It is the weekly Cloud Chart of the S&P 500 has just crossed the cloud into bullish territory. This chart has been an extremely reliable roadmap for the market over the last twenty years with only four transitions through the cloud. On the basis of these signals, you would have sold the US stock market in mid 2000, bought in mid 2003, sold in mid 2008 and bought again in late 2009. In each case the signals were later than the tops and bottoms, but we know that Cloud Charts are a trend following technique which will call the turning points in markets retrospectively.

Chart 12-3: 2% log scale Point and Figure chart for S&P 500 Index

If these were the only four calls you made as a Fund Manager on Wall Street in the last twenty years you would be considered something of a guru in financial markets.

It is worth noting that the last cloud cross on this weekly chart below was a long way from the low point in price. This is for two reasons. The first reason is that markets fell so precipitously in 2008 that it took a long time for the cloud to catch up and the distance between the price and the cloud was very great. The speed of collapse in prices was much greater than in 2001 as we can see on this chart. Secondly the corresponding speed of recovery from the lows was also great, meaning that prices didn't wander sideways through the cloud in the way they did in 2003. This highlights a weakness of Cloud Charts in that they don't always deal so well with a dramatic V shaped recovery. We have established the clouds also don't work so well in sideways markets. Consequently they work best if the trend is not too steep and not too shallow in what we might consider to be normal trending behaviour. As highlighted previously if the clouds are hard to read, due to the extremes of steepness, it is best to switch to another time frame. We will see shortly how the daily chart in this case was much clearer.

Chart 12-4: Weekly Cloud Chart for S&P 500 Index with cloud crosses marked

Now that the lagging line is through the cloud on the weekly chart, we will need to watch for signs of confirmation of the new trend in the weeks and months ahead. The zoomed chart below shows trend lines drawn roughly across the cloud top and cloud base. We would expect to see the price and the lagging line interacting with these, recognising we could pull back into the cloud by as much as 200 points and still be in the new bull trend. If the price does stay above 1,050 points in the months ahead (even 1,000 six months out) then the lagging line will still be very much in positive territory. A fall of the index through 900 points would be a sign of a failed recovery. Most of all if we can break above 1,150 points on this chart we would have a 'higher high' confirming the recovery was well in train.

Chart 12-5: Weekly Cloud Chart for S&P 500 Index with support lines of cloud

To gain an idea of price points where the current recovery in markets might experience some resistance, we can look at the Fibonacci retracement (top chart next page) from the 2007 high to the 2009 low. We see the market did find support on the 23.6% level before jumping to the important 38.2% and pausing again. We have broken through the 50% rule of thumb before coming back below it and prices may seesaw around this mark of about 1,120 points. The fact that levels have bounded the price quite closely in the recovery so far gives us some confidence that resistance is likely at the renowned 61.8% mark, here around 1,230 points, should we break above 1,150 to new highs. We should also expect the 38.2% level to provide support at around 1,115 points, were we to see another setback in the market. The weekly cloud levels in the previous chart have been left on this chart to provide an appreciation of the boundaries for the price to stay above in the new bullish zone above the cloud top.

Chart 12-6: Weekly chart for S&P 500 Index with cloud support lines and Fibonacci retracements

## Medium term

The long term picture of the US market has only recently turned bullish, but the medium term picture, as represented by the daily Cloud Chart below, has been bullish for some months. Here we see how the transition occurred in April 2009 with some interaction between the price and the cloud in the months that followed. This chart is now at an interesting juncture with the price having moved below the cloud and entered the cloud from below and the cloud spans having themselves crossed as signified by the red shading at the end. The lagging line is the key here, having bounced off the cloud at 1,075 points and then having fallen temporarily through the cloud, we are now once more above the cloud. We need to be vigilant as prices are in this testing area, but the trend is still bullish. The recent high of 1,150 and low of 1,050 may act as a range on prices in the coming weeks which would mean more noisy signals with the cloud as it moves sideways.

Chart 12-7: Daily Cloud Chart for S&P 500 Index

Looking at the medium term using a Point and Figure Chart, we are best to start with our 'rule of thumb' 1% of the price as our box size. This gives us a 10 x 3 arithmetic chart as shown below. Here we are in an uptrend with an internal line of support being heavily tested as prices move up. This chart is unequivocally bullish. We see how well the vertical targets have worked in the past with the downside targets of 820 and 880 points that were given at around 1,200 points being met. We also see the upside target of 1,130 points given at 850 points from the vertical thrust from the low in the market was also met and slightly exceeded. This is bullish confirmation. We have a new upside target of 1,270 points which has been activated and we also have a new counter-trend downside target of 880 points. This target would be activated with a close below 1,060 points and would be negated completely with a move to a new high. For now the target of 1,270 in line with the trend should be favoured.

Chart 12-8: Daily 10 x 3 Point and Figure chart for S&P 500 Index

While the medium picture still looks fairly bullish for the US stock market, the seasonality chart below shows that stocks have not performed well at the start of the year recently. This seasonal chart takes the moves of the previous 10 years into account and projects an average forward. The chart changes each year with the benefit of the previous year in the new calculation for the year ahead. In the last few years stocks have fallen and several years ago they were going sideways with the performance nearly always being in the second half of the year. The market may go sideways for longer on the basis of this chart.

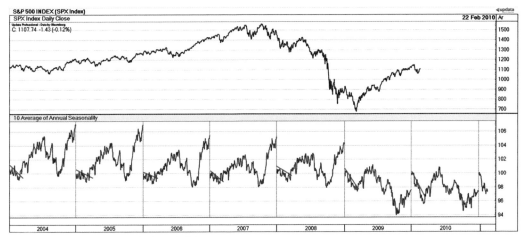

Chart 12-9: Daily seasonal chart for S&P 500 Index

With the recent sell off in the market and a potential sideways move in the US stock market, a quick check of the On Balance Volume reassures us that heavy selling has not been happening. The volume trend is still up here as the 55 day moving average of OBV shows.

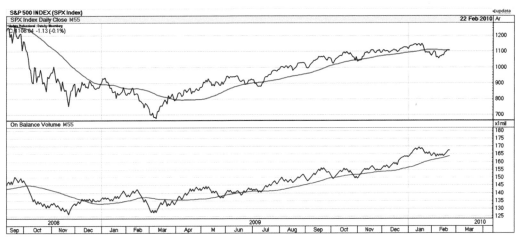

Chart 12-10: Daily chart for S&P 500 Index with On Balance Volume

## Short term

The hourly Cloud Chart shows us the short term picture for the S&P 500 Index. Here we see the cloud being crossed in November and the commencement of a new uptrend. Sideways price congestion in December did make this chart hard to read before there was a break to a new high and the market started trending again. Around the middle of January, the uptrend ended with a cloud cross and a new short term downtrend began. Prices bottomed a little higher than the low we saw in November, itself a bullish sign, and the cloud has now been crossed to the upside decisively by the price and lagging line. From this chart, the short term picture for the market is bullish.

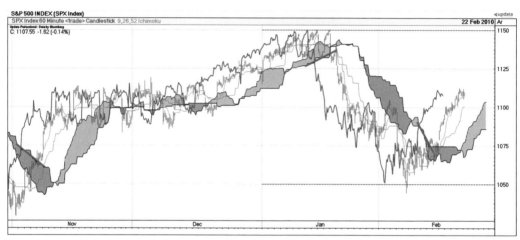

Chart 12-11: 60 minute Cloud Chart for S&P 500 Index

The shorter term picture on the 5 x 3 Point and Figure Chart shows an uptrend is in place. A target at 1,130 (as per the 10 x 3 chart) which has been exceeded, confirms bullish action. We have a series of upside targets off three separate buying thrusts at 1,225, 1,250 and 1,270 points. However, there is a downside count target of 925 points which is an activated counter trend target. Given this and the fact that there are three upside targets, due to more long columns of X's in the uptrend, we would apply less importance to this target. However, this downside price target does hang over us until we see a new high above 1,150 at which point it would be negated and removed from the chart.

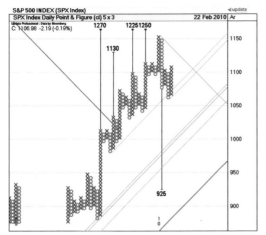

Chart 12-12: Daily 5 x 3 Point and Figure chart for S&P 500 Index

Looking at some indicators on the short term chart below we see Fibonacci retracement levels taken from the January high to the February low. The levels have not provided such clear points of resistance and support, but we have retraced more than 50% of the move and are now nudging resistance seen a couple of weeks earlier. The 14 period RSI has given relatively good signals at the 30 and 70 levels as marked, although the one given towards the end of January when the price was consolidating was not so good. The move to lower levels or an optimised long stop-loss would have alerted us to a failed signal and saved us from a big loss in this case. The RSI is now heading into the overbought region on this chart, but the optimised stop-losses shown will allow us to stay in if prices run higher still.

Chart 12-13: 60 minute chart for S&P 500 Index, with stop-losses, Fibonacci retracements and RSI

The 60 minute cloud chart is bullish and looking at a 1 minute 1 x 3 Point and Figure Chart we see three upside targets given off the lows during the recovery in prices have been met. While this is bullish confirmation, the lack of further significant upside targets suggest that the market may be overbought short term. The picture is bullish here as well, but there are no clear signs of a good buying opportunity on this time horizon.

Chart 12-14: One minute 1 x 3 Point and Figure chart for S&P 500 Index with price targets

## Very short term

The very short term picture for the market can be studied with a 10 minute Cloud Chart as shown below. This is also a bullish chart, but we see the noise on this chart several days ago in the sideways range and this prompts us to explore an adjacent time frame.

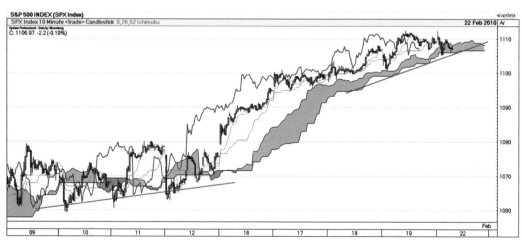

Chart 12-15: 10 minute Cloud Chart for S&P 500 Index

On the next page we see the 15 minute chart with the same support lines drawn on. This time frame tended to bound the price moves better several days ago and as a result may be a better time frame for the very short term time horizon.

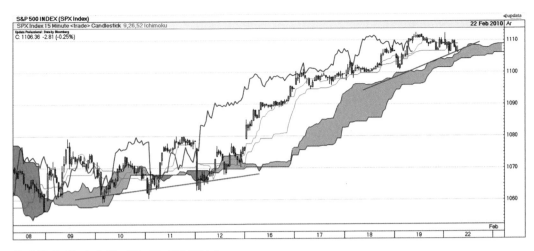

Chart 12-16: 15 minute Cloud Chart for S&P 500 Index

## Stock Analysis

The analysis conducted on the US stock market above can just as easily be carried out on another instrument such as a currency or a commodity, but here we will look at a US stock, Travelers, an Insurance company, one of the thirty members of the Dow Jones Industrial Average Index.

### Very long term

The very long term monthly Cloud Chart of Travelers shows the stock has been a steady long term performer over decades, with the price almost entirely above the cloud. While there have been a couple of breaches of the monthly cloud by lagging line, we see two very clear touches on the cloud base marked. There is potentially a very large consolidation pattern in the form of an ascending triangle and, if the stock breaks to a new high, prices could run in the space of a year or so as quickly as they did a decade ago.

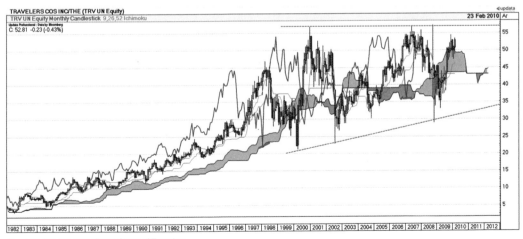

Chart 12-17: Monthly Cloud Chart of Travelers

The zoomed monthly chart below shows the monthly MACD and MACD Histogram and we see that the MACD has given relatively good signals. The MACD Histogram has worked well at the extremes.

Chart 12-18: Monthly chart of Travelers with MACD and MACD Histogram

## Long term

The long term picture as shown with the weekly chart below shows how 2008 was a year to avoid being invested in Travelers stock. In the middle of 2009, prices did recover entering a new long term bull phase, now leaving scope for the stock to break to a new all time high.

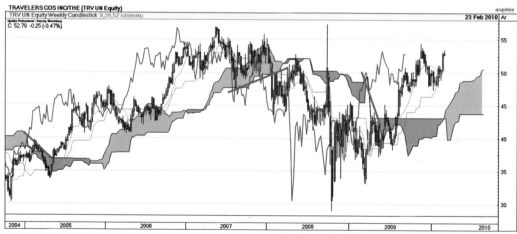

Chart 12-19: Weekly Cloud Chart of Travelers

The long term 1 x 3 arithmetic Point and Figure Chart (next page), at around 2% of the price now, shows two upside targets to $61. The trend is up, but with the sideways range of the last ten years, the trend has chopped and changed such that it is hard to say whether this new uptrend will hold. We see multiple lines of support now, but the real sign of a sustainable uptrend will be a move to new highs above $57.

The fact that we have price targets 'clustering' at $61 off two buying thrusts from lows several months apart, does suggest that the stock could break to these all time price levels.

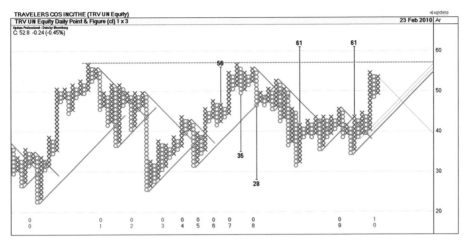

Chart 12-20: Daily 1 x 3 Point and Figure chart of Travelers

## Medium term

The medium term, daily, Cloud Chart of Travelers shows the price and the lagging line above the cloud in recent months, although a breach of the cloud has occurred recently. The move back above the cloud is encouraging, but seeing prices make a new high above the November 2009 high would provide more comfort in the medium term time frame.

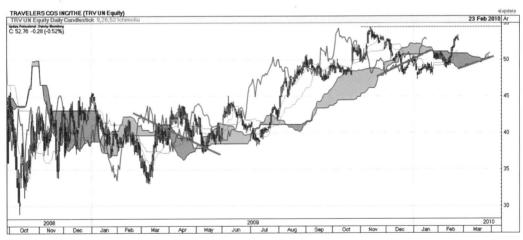

Chart 12-21: Daily Cloud Chart of Travelers

The daily line chart below shows a Relative Strength and an On Balance Volume chart. The relative strength is against the S&P 500 Index, normalised to 100 at the start of 2008. From this chart we see that Travelers ran in-line with the US stock market through most of 2008 as the relative chart went sideways. In the last few months of 2008, Travelers outperformed the market by 40% (140 on y-axis) which was mainly down to the stock holding its price in a falling market overall. Since the beginning of 2009, the stock has slightly underperformed the market as the trend channel (least squares regression) on the relative chart shows, but over two years the stock has outperformed the market by 30%, demonstrating inherent strength.

The On Balance Volume chart has been in line with the price over the last couple of years but is now close to making new highs when the price is not. This suggests that more buying is occurring on up days with less selling on down days. This is not a strong example of divergence, but it does demonstrate some clever accumulation of the stock favouring prices going higher still.

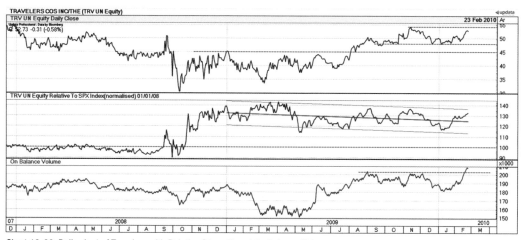

Chart 12-22: Daily chart of Travelers with Relative Strength and On Balance Volume

The medium term Point and Figure Chart on the next page, uses a 'rule of thumb 1% of the price, $0.5 x 3 box size, shows an uptrend position. There are upside targets to $55 and $57, right on previous levels of resistance. There is an activated downside target of $37.5, a counter-trend target which would be negated with a new high at $55. This medium term time frame chart is unequivocally bullish.

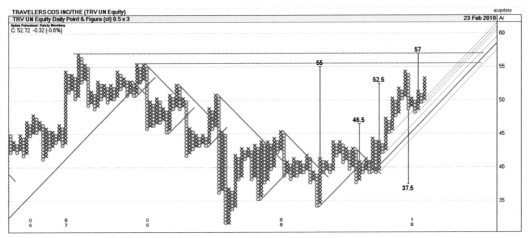

Chart 12-23: Daily 0.5 x 3 Point and Figure chart of Travelers

### Short term

The short term 60 minute chart shows the move to a bearish state in November followed by a long sideways ranging bottom in December and January. Prices did break out of this range and into bullish territory in February and are now a long way from the cloud.

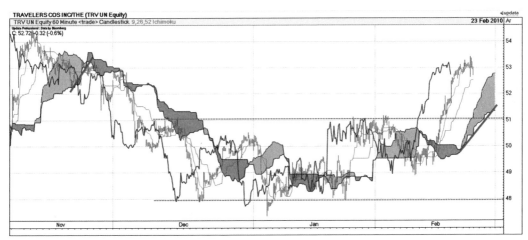

Chart 12-24: 60 minute Cloud Chart of Travelers

The 60 minute Candlestick chart below shows long and short optimised stop-losses of 0.8% and 1.55% respectively. The 14 period RSI has given relatively good signals as marked on the RSI, but the RSI is also higher than it has been at any time in the last few months on the hourly chart suggesting that prices are overbought short term. The bottom window shows a 40 hour correlation between Travelers and the S&P 500 Index. We see on a short term basis currently that the stock is highly correlated to the market. This correlation has been negative at times in January, i.e. the stock moves have been in the opposite direction to the market. The correlation is a strong sign of a market following stock now, but we shouldn't be surprised to see this relationship changing in the days ahead. The short term picture is one of bullishness, but with a high risk of the stock being overbought on this time horizon.

Chart 12-25: 60 minute chart of Travelers with RSI and 40 hour correlation to S&P 500 Index

The 10 cent x 3 chart shows that prices have broken out with an upside potential of $56.80. The risk reward ratio on this trade with a stop price of $51.10 is 2.5, making it a fairly favourable trade.

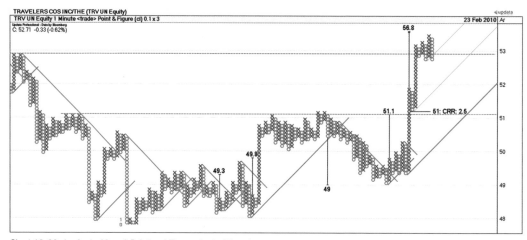

Chart 12-26: 1 minute 10c x 3 Point and Figure chart of Travelers

## Very short term

The very short term 10 minute Cloud Chart highlights the strength of the trend in the last few trading sessions. A cross of this cloud would highlight a clear end to the very short term trend. This would require the lagging line to move below $51.80 in the hours ahead on this chart.

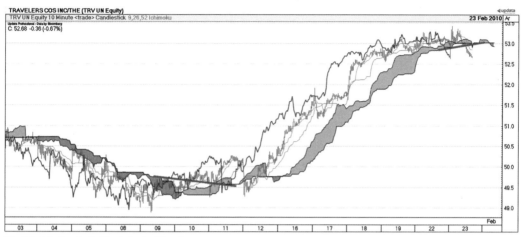

Chart 12-27: 10 minute Cloud Chart of Travelers

The very short term targets on the 0.025 x 3 chart show targets met and further upside which is also a bullish picture.

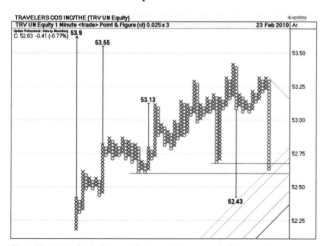

Chart 12-28: 1 minute 2.5c x 3 Point and Figure chart of Traveler8

Overall the picture on Travelers is bullish on nearly all time horizons, though some time frames are offering better trade entry opportunities than others.

It is a useful exercise to summarise the analysis we have conducted:

## S&P 500 Index – The market

### Very long term – Monthly – Time Horizon: a few years
Cloud is bearish, need to break 1,400 by end of 2010 to turn bullish. Big sideways range in the price, new all time high above 1,550 needed for a new long term bull market. Long term buy signals have been given on a number of monthly indicators. There is a very long term upside target of 1,780 points.

### Long term - Weekly – Time Horizon: several months
Just crossing into bullish territory now, with the lagging line crossing the cloud. Three very reliable signals have been given on this chart in the last decade. The price is able to pull back up 200 points and stay bullish above the cloud. The market is testing the 50% Fibonacci retracement now as it rises. The next level is at around 1,230 points. We may see resistance here.

### Medium term – Daily – Time Horizon: several weeks
The cloud gave a buy signal in spring 2009 and markets have risen strongly since. A sideways range of 1,050 – 1,150 looks to be developing. Breaking either of these levels will govern the next direction for the market medium term. There is an activated upside target of 1,270 and a non activated counter trend target of 880 points. The Point and Figure chart favours the upside, though seasonal studies show us that stocks have not performed well at this time in recent years. The On Balance Volume chart confirms the uptrend.

### Short term - Hourly – Time Horizon: several days
The cloud on the 60 minute chart has just seen a bullish cross, suggesting we are moving back to the top of the 1,150 range. There are short term upside targets of 1,225, 1,250 and 1,270 which outweigh a countertrend target of 925 points. The RSI is suggesting short term overbought, but the price has made it through the major Fib levels in this recovery.

### Very Short Term – 10 minute – Time Horizon: several hours
The very short term cloud is bullish but being tested. A very short term sell signal would be given with a move below 1,105, but the level it would be given at is rising. The 10 minute chart has given a few false signals and the 15 minute chart seems to be performing better at the moment. Not much by way of upside targets in the very short term.

## The Travelers Companies Inc – The stock

### Very long term – Monthly – Time Horizon: a few years
Cloud is bullish, spectacularly long term uptrend. Possible ascending triangle, need a new all time high of $57 for price to really run. Indicators giving long term buy signals.

### Long term - Weekly – Time Horizon: several months
Cloud is bullish with a cross in 2009 leaving scope to break to a new all time high. Two long term targets clustering at $61 suggest quite a high likelihood of this target area being met, once price makes a new high.

**Medium term – Daily – Time Horizon: several weeks**
Cloud is bullish after a cross in early 2009. Has been tested recently with a short breach, but is positive again. November high of just under $55 needs to be broken for uptrend to continue medium term. On Balance Volume suggests investors are accumulating the stock. The relative performance to the market is not strong and needs watching. Medium term targets of $55 and $57 with a countertrend target of $37.50 but very strong uptrend support on the Point and Figure Chart.

**Short term - Hourly – Time Horizon: several days**
The stock is bullish on the cloud with a move out of a congested trading range. Short term sell currently below $51.50. RSI suggesting overbought. Optimised stop-loss of 1.55% working well and Travelers is highly correlated to the market short term at the moment. Short Term target of $56.80.

**Very short term – 10 minute – Time Horizon: several hours**
The cloud has just been crossed to the downside suggesting a setback in the very short term with a bearish picture. A downside target of $52.43 was given around $52.10. With the price now at $52.63, there is possibly little downside left. Upside targets of $53.55 and $53.90 remain in train once new highs are made in the very short term.

## Summary points

- Analysis will be more rigorous with a blend of techniques
- It is always good to break analysis down into time horizons
- Start very long term first and work down to the shorter term
- With stocks, analysing the market first is a good idea
- Start with the clouds as they are the immediate roadmap for the time frame
- Summarising your analysis will increase your overall understanding

# Summary of Part 2

The previous five chapters should provide you with a complete overview of how to apply Cloud Charts to your own trading and investing. This section of the book alone should be enough to get the experienced user of charts up and running with the Cloud Chart technique.

## What we have learned

In Chapter 8 we covered the construction of Cloud Charts. It is good to know and understand the construction of the charts off by heart to get the most value from the charts. You should know the numbers 9, 26 and 52 and be able to recall them. One way to do this is to think; 9 is 1 less than 10, 26 weeks is half a year, 52 weeks is one year. The turning and standard lines are calculated from the midpoints of the highest high and lowest low for the first two periods 9 and 26. Cloud span A is the midpoint of these two lines shifted forward 26 bars. Cloud span B uses the last of the three periods, 52, and is also shifted forward 26 bars. Last of all the lagging line is the price line shifted back 26 bars. Remember the offset is always the same, 26 bars. It is worth configuring your charts in such a way that they are easy for you to understand at a glance. This will come down to personal preference.

Chapter 9 deals with the interpretation of Cloud Charts. While you will find references on how they are constructed, there is very little documentation in English available on how they are read and analysed. This section addresses this for the first time. The basic idea is that prices above the cloud are bullish and prices below the cloud are bearish. If prices are in the cloud it is the direction which they entered that governs the trend state. From above is bullish, from below is bearish. The most important signal is the lagging line crossing the cloud. Price crossing the cloud is an early warning signal. Look for the price and lagging line touching the edges of the cloud confirming support or resistance depending on the trend state. The turning and standard lines crossing each other can be a useful shorter term signal when prices are a long way from the cloud.

The cloud is unique in that it is projected forward which gives us valuable thinking time ahead of the price. Normally we will spot the trend direction in an instant based on the colour of the cloud at the far right of the chart. Cloud Charts provide you with a trading roadmap. If we are above the cloud we are bullish and we are looking for trading opportunities to go long. If we are below the cloud we are bearish and looking for trading opportunities to go short. This roadmap should help us to avoid trading big positions against the trend. One drawback with Cloud Charts is that they don't work very well in sideways or range bound markets.

Chapter 10 is one of the most important chapters in the book. The multiple time frame analysis can be conducted with any technical analysis technique and the same rules would apply, but Cloud Charts almost force us to explore other time frames to see the full picture. Always ask yourself 'What's my Time Horizon?' and make sure you are looking at the right charts to match the answer to your question.

Consider using a Trading Time Horizon Table, so you don't get confused on the various time frames and what they mean. Multiple time frame charts can be viewed on the same screen to give you an overview across time horizons at a glance and in Chapter 11 we conduct a multiple time frame analysis of Oil as a worked example. Towards the end of Chapter 11 we look at pointers to help us understand when we should be looking up a time frame or down a time frame.

We look at Japanese Pattern Techniques in Chapter 11 via the ideas of wave principle, price targets and time span. The price patterns follow the letters I, V, N, P and Y and combinations of these. We explore key numbers as set out in the Japanese texts on Ichimoku charting. In this chapter we show how Cloud Charts already have price and time targets effectively built in. The forward nature of the cloud always gives us a 26 bar projection ahead. The cloud will always be telling us about either an area of support or an area of resistance depending on the trend state defined by the cloud. Adjacent time frame charts can also provide us with additional information on support and resistance to be used as price targets on the chart we are studying.

The final chapter in Part 2 is a full worked example of analysing a US stock market index and a major US stock. This chapter shows you how to use the well known technical analysis techniques covered in Part 1 of the book with the Cloud Chart techniques learned in Part 2. No single technique can be completely relied upon and your analysis will be stronger if you use a blend of techniques. From these worked examples we can see how Cloud Charts give us an excellent initial perspective on each time frame. The chart analysis example conducted in this chapter allows us to ascertain the outlook for prices across a series of time horizons. You should now be in a position to carry out a similar analysis exercise on other instruments yourself.

# Part 3 - **Advanced Cloud Chart Techniques**

---

*Advance, and never halt, for advancing is perfection*

Kahlil Gibran 1883-1931

# Chapter 13 - **Ichimoku Indicator Techniques**

In the previous chapter we looked at using Cloud Charts alongside other technical analysis techniques. Now we will look at ways to combine the techniques such that the resulting tools are hybrid charts of clouds and standard analysis tools. This combines the ideas we learned in Part 1 with the Cloud Chart techniques form Part 2.

Students of the subject often ask if other cloud construction periods can be used. We will look at optimisation of the periods in the next chapter, but here we see the effects of changing the 9, 26 and 52 periods. The Fibonacci numbers, 8, 21, 55 used, shown in the top window make little difference in the chart appearance versus the standard periods.

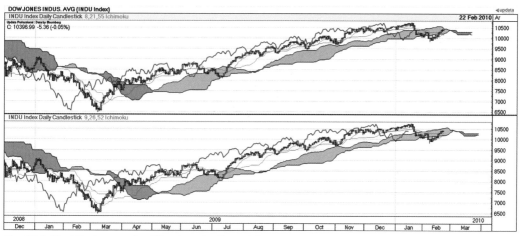

Chart 13-1: Cloud Charts comparing different construction periods

Move to periods further away though, such as 5,13, 34 in the top window and we see that chart differences start to appear. You may get a slightly earlier signal, as with the bullish cross in March 2009 but you also had a failed signal in December 2008 with the shorter signals, which was avoided with the standard 9,26 and 52 periods.

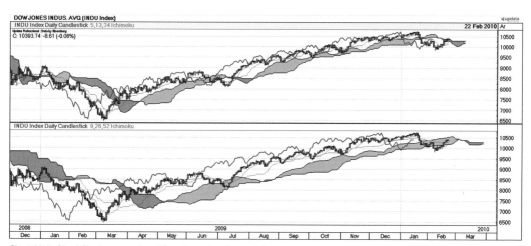

Chart 13-2: Cloud Charts comparing different construction periods

It is easy to assume that, by shortening the construction periods, you can gain an edge with earlier signals over other traders. But shortening the construction periods will not necessarily do this. Here we see how on a 5 minute chart the lagging line signal was later when the shorter 8, 21, 34 periods were used. The price crossed below the cloud earlier, but we see all sort of things change such as cloud thickness and where other crosses occur. If you want to get an earlier signal than the 5 minute chart it would better to stick to the 9, 26, 52 periods and use a shorter term chart.

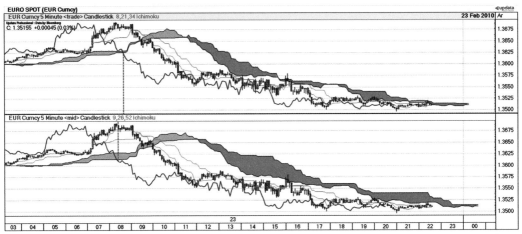

Chart 13-3: Cloud Charts comparing different construction period signals

It is also possible to use 'tick' candles for the construction of Cloud Charts. This is where the candles are not a number of minutes wide, but are instead a number of 'ticks' or trades wide. This can be good for trading less liquid instruments. Here we see a 5 Tick chart for a European power contract. This is one way to deal with irregular price updates.

Chart 13-4: Cloud Chart of German Power with 5 tick bars

Changing the cloud construction periods is one of the biggest debates among followers of the Ichimoku technique. Proving there is better period combination across all instrument sets that you are likely to encounter is fraught with difficulty. What may work for a stock may not for a commodity and vice versa. We learned in Part 2 that Cloud Charts are not so successful in sideways markets, and no matter how much you change the 9, 26 and 52 construction periods this will still be the case. Most traders will be interested in intra-day charts and here we can set the time frame by varying number of minutes for the chart bars until we see visually which time frame gives the best signals. Unless you are experienced with optimisation and back-testing, it is recommended you stick with the standard construction periods.

One thing we can do with the construction is to extend the cloud a little further by making the assumption that no new highs or lows will occur going forward. First consider cloud span B which is constructed from the midpoint of the high and low across the last 52 bars. Let us consider the next bar, we know that the price 52 sessions ago drops out of the calculation and if that price was not the highest high or lowest low and neither is the new incoming bar, then the cloud span B value will not change. On this basis we can continue to calculate cloud span B for another 52 bars by looking back 51, 50, 49....for the midpoint of the highest high and lowest low until there is no data left. This can be done similarly for cloud span A by with the 26 period using 25, 24, 23....and the 9 period using 9, 8, 7...until there is only one bar left in each case to continue running with cloud span 2. After 26 periods, cloud span A will run sideways at the level of the midpoint of the high and low of the very last price candle.

This resulting extended cloud will look like this if prices don't change for the next 52 bars. This is of course a big assumption to make and this extended cloud would look very different with new dramatic price changes. Having an idea of where the cloud will go further out can be useful, especially on shorter term time frames and although it isn't strictly correct it will adjust with the new price information anyway. The chart below shows the cloud extended on the basis of this construction.

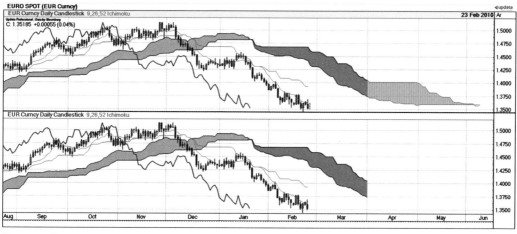

Chart 13-5: Cloud Charts of Eurodollar with Cloud extended

## Moving Averages

It might be possible to arrive at some useful indicators by applying the standard techniques we learned in Part 1 to the cloud. Here we see a 26 day moving average which is calculated from the midpoint values from the cloud each day.

Chart 13-6: 26 period average of cloud midpoints

This can be taken a step further using OBOS, the distance between the price and the average. Here we have a 1 day average, which gives us the middle of the cloud and the OBOS showing the distance between the price and the cloud centre.

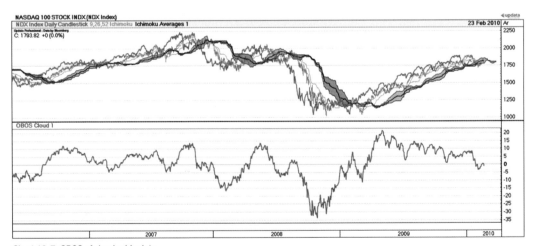

Chart 13-7: OBOS of cloud midpoints

If we want to understand how the width of the cloud might impact the future direction of prices this might be best done with an indicator which draws the cloud width. Here we see this shown below in the lower window for the FTSE 100 Index with the price overlaid. From this we can see that when the cloud is unusually wide, as marked, the price does seem to become exhausted a couple of months after. This indicator could provide a useful warning in future.

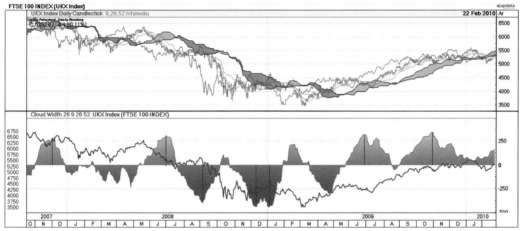

Chart 13-8: Cloud Width for FTSE 100 Index with price overlaid

The chart below shows 26 week cloud momentum for the Dax Index, where we measure the midpoint of the cloud versus 26 weeks ago. This may also help us to understand areas of price exhaustion which tends to occur at the extremes when we relate it back historically. A 21 period average of this momentum could be used for signals at the extremes as shown.

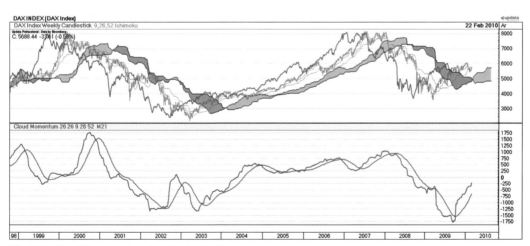

Chart 13-9: Cloud Momentum based on cloud midpoints

## Clouds of Relative Strength and Spread Charts

We can use Cloud Charts on relative strength charts in addition to charts of price. Here we see a chart of Microsoft relative to the S&P 500 Index with a cloud applied. The signal of the relative strength line and its lagging line crossing the cloud is given after a long relative outperformance.

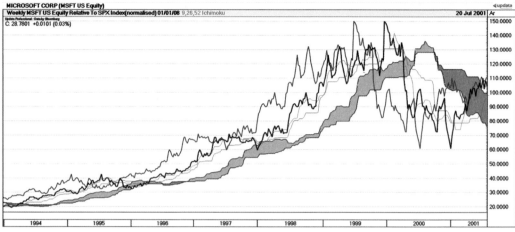

Chart 13-10: Cloud Chart of Relative Strength

Cloud Charts can also be helpful in identifying the turning points on a spread chart. Here we see a Spark Spread for electricity, gas and emissions with the cloud applied. This could be done as easily on a stock pair or any other spread to identify when the relationship is changing.

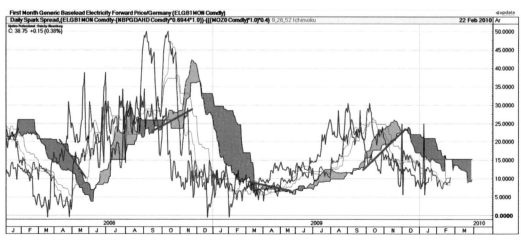

Chart 13-11: Cloud Chart of a Spark Spread

## Clouds of Point and Figure charts

In the previous chapter we looked at swapping between Cloud Charts and Point and Figure charts. Here we see a Cloud Chart of a Point and Figure chart. The cloud is constructed on the column highs and lows looking back 9, 26 and 52 columns.

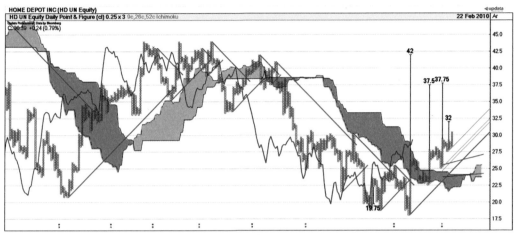

Chart 13-12: Cloud Chart constructed from a Point Figure chart of Home Depot

The chart above alters the Cloud Chart to match the Point and Figure. Another possibility would be to look at how the Point and Figure columns are represented on the cloud. Below we see the price colour coded for up columns (blue) and down columns (red) accordingly.

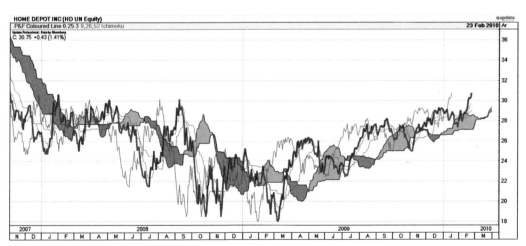

Chart 13-13: Point and Figure columns represented on a Cloud Chart

## Clouds Charts and Volume

Candle Volume charts can also be used with Cloud Charts. Here we see one for Intel Corp. The cloud on each day will be the width of the candle of that day, but in all other aspects the analysis is the same. This is one of the best ways to incorporate volume into your Cloud Charts and we see at the end of this chart that the selloffs and temporary cloud breaches have occurred on heavy volume.

Chart 13-14: Cloud Chart for Intel with CandleVolume

Flipping the chart was a method we covered for removing your inherent bias at the end of Chapter 4. This applies perfectly well to Cloud Charts as we see here for a chart of the NASDAQ 100 with all elements of the cloud inverted. From this chart, can we see a recovery as a result of a cloud cross? If so we are saying we can see a breakdown of the uptrend.

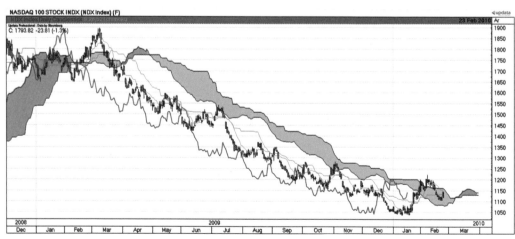

Chart 13-15: Cloud Chart for NASDAQ 100 Index inverted or 'flipped'

Last of all in Part 1, we looked at trailing stop-losses. The cloud base is effectively a trailing stop which has been projected ahead of the price. Here we see cloud span 2 highlighted and performing much the same function as a trailing stop-loss.

Chart 13-16: Cloud Chart for NASDAQ 100 index with cloud base as a stop-loss

The blue line in the chart below is the same stop-loss as the cloud base above. Because the lagging line is the price shifted back 26 bars, we can effectively create a lagging line stop (red below) for the price by shifting the cloud base forward 26 bars. When the price falls through the lower stop on this chart, that would be the point at which the lagging line is falling below the cloud. The green line in the lower window is the distance between the lagging stop and the price. This crosses the zero line when the lagging line crosses the cloud. At the end of the chart it shows the distance from the cloud narrowing, effectively diverging from the price trend which is a warning that the speed of prices increasing is slowing down.

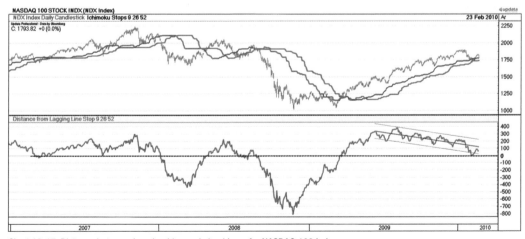

Chart 13-17: Distance between Lagging Line and cloud base for NASDAQ 100 Index

The charts in this chapter show you some additional ways to apply Cloud Charts. Some of these lines are written with simple programming and the code for these can be downloaded at cloudcharts.com. Some of these ideas also lead us to look at back-testing and trading strategies in the next chapter.

## Summary points

- You can use numbers such as Fibonacci for the construction but it is not recommended if you are new to back-testing and optimisation
- You can extend the cloud on the basis prices won't change from the last price
- You can create moving averages of the cloud midpoints
- An Overbought/Oversold (OBOS) indicator can tell us the price distance from the cloud to understand where prices have potentially moved to far from the cloud
- The width of the cloud as an indicator might provide clues to price exhaustion
- The momentum of the cloud itself can be calculated to see speed of trend changing
- Cloud Charts on relative strength and spread charts as well and can help to show turning points in these lines
- Cloud Charts can be constructed on Point and Figure columns
- CandleVolume will bring volume into a Cloud Chart
- Cloud trailing stop-losses can provide a useful exit tool

# Chapter 14 - **Back-testing and Trading Strategies**

One of the most common questions that students of Cloud Charts ask is 'Have you back-tested the technique?' Cloud Charts require a degree of subjective interpretation which can make quantitative back-testing with hard coded criteria challenging. Back-testing, sometimes known as system testing, can be done by programming certain entry and exit criteria and seeing the overall trading results. Covering the subject area in great detail is beyond the scope of this book and this chapter is designed to show you some basic findings from simple back-test results surrounding Cloud Charts. This is a rapidly growing area of computerised trading and to keep abreast of it in reference to Cloud Charts, visit cloudcharts.com.

## Stop and Reverse systems

Towards the end of Chapter 7, we looked at how money management based trading tools such as Optimised Stop-losses and Parabolic SAR produced better overall profit results by keeping losses small. The chart below shows an Optimised Stop-loss, stop and reverse system, in this case on Eurodollar. This 'Flip-Flop Stop-loss' system is based around the idea that you exit a long position when a long trailing stop-loss is breached, and you then enter a short position until the short stop is breached swapping you back to long. This system is designed to keep you the right side of any big move such that you are running a profit, while keeping losses small when the instrument is non-trending. The secret is the optimisation of the stop percentages, as we explored in Chapter 7. Here we see, for the Euro, that 2.7% long and 2.3% short stop-losses produced the optimum results with the Equity Line in the lower window showing the growth in capital with this strategy.

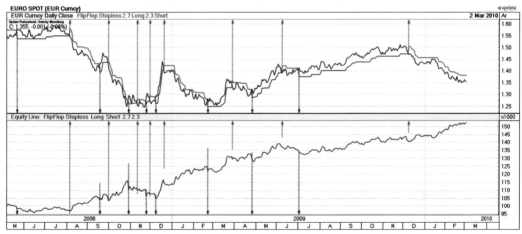

Chart 14-1: Flipflop stop-loss tested with equity line for Eurodollar

In the previous chapter we looked at Cloud Stop-losses which were based on Cloud Span A with the price and the lagging line crossing for an exit signal. Unlike the trailing stop-losses we looked at in Chapter 7, Cloud Stop-losses are not suited to an optimised percentage. Variability in where the cloud stop would give a signal may be created by altering a number of elements of the cloud construction.

## Signal Delay

The cloud construction periods of 9, 26 and 52 could be optimised by testing adjacent periods which we will explore in this chapter. The 26 bar offset of the cloud could be optimised and the offset of the lagging line from the price could also be optimised. Do we take the trading signal on the price crossing the cloud or the lagging line crossing? And, as with stop-losses, should we wait a number of bars after a cross? With three periods, two offsets (three if we optimise each cloud span offset), two potential signals and one signal delay, we end up with eight variables. If we chose to optimise a range, of say ten surrounding increments, for each of the periods, and also the offsets and the signal delay we will have over a million calculations per instrument. We might also choose a universe of several hundred instruments to reach some conclusions on the best combinations to use. Run these optimisations across years of data, several thousand data points, and you have an awful lot of data processing on your hands.

So this means that back-testing the Cloud Chart technique is a non-trivial exercise and across a large universe we would not expect any optimised test results for the variables to be normally distributed about a mean value. We will see this later in this chapter. Realistically it is best to decide which variables stay fixed and which might be worth optimising. Given that the technique is predominantly subjective, fixing the signals is a good place to start in order to conduct some tests. The chart below shows a simple back-test of the price crossing the cloud for the Euro. A buy signal (long entry, short exit) is a close above the cloud, where the last 'price outside cloud position' was below the cloud. A sell signal (long exit, short entry) is where the price crosses below the cloud, with the last 'price outside cloud condition' below the cloud. The lower window shows the equity curve for this strategy where there were only four trades across a year.

Chart 14-2: Cloud Chart of Eurodollar with signals given

The first trade on this chart occurred at point A. The price closed above the cloud for just one day and that was enough for the mathematical rules of the system, which has no subjective capability, to go long and buy. Was this a buy signal through the cloud? Strictly speaking it was, but using the subjective interpretation of Cloud Charts covered in Part 2, we would be unlikely to accept it as a signal to buy.

At point B, the price closes below the cloud, and a few days later it closes above the cloud again. Deploying a 'signal delay' would have allowed us to avoid the first two trades with a better single entry at B.

Running the system again and testing waiting a day, two days, and so on up to five days we find that we only need to have waited an extra day in this instance to avoid the first two signals. In both cases we only closed outside the cloud for a day. We also see that our equity line in the chart below is improved versus the previous chart, by simply waiting a day. As we saw in Chapter 7, there might be a price/time conundrum where you wouldn't wait a day if the breach was significant. This could be built into a Cloud Chart trading system to further improve results.

Chart 14-3: Cloud Chart of Eurodollar with signals eliminated with signal delay

If we are using the lagging line crossing the cloud as our signal the same signal delay method may be applied. The chart below shows two temporary breaches on the lagging line at A and B, marked with vertical lines because the actual trades will occur 26 bars forward where the price is at that time.

Chart 14-4: Cloud Chart with Lagging Line tested without signal delay

The chart below shows, having optimised the signal delay, that waiting three days before accepting the lagging line breach would have removed the signals at A and B. At C the lagging line found support on the cloud in the normal way. We see the steady trend in the equity line showing our capital is growing while the underlying instrument is not trending so clearly.

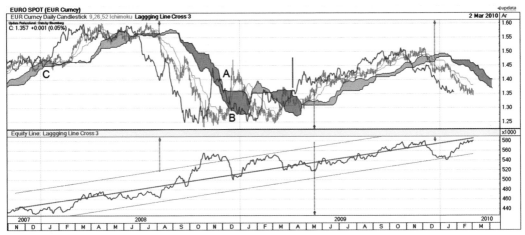

Chart 14-5: Cloud Chart with Lagging Line tested with signal delay

This exercise can be conducted across a universe of instruments. Optimising a signal delay for the lagging line crossing the cloud, between 0 and 5 days for the S&P 500 Index constituent stocks we get a results screen as below.

Figure 14-1: Results screen from system testing for the best signal delay to use for S&P 500 stocks

The test was conducted over the last five years for every stock establishing which signal delay worked best for each individual stock and the results were:

| Signal Delay | Number of Stocks | Percentage of Stocks |
|:---:|:---:|:---:|
| 0 | 102 | 20 |
| 1 | 74 | 15 |
| 2 | 71 | 14 |
| 3 | 72 | 15 |
| 4 | 77 | 15 |
| 5 | 104 | 21 |

Figure 14-2: Results for best signal delay on S&P 500 stocks

We can see from this that there is no preponderance towards any one signal delay period and that they are evenly spread with no clear answer for the best signal delay to use. This highlights the subjectivity needed to properly interpret Cloud Charts. You need to look at previous breaches for a given instrument and judge the best signal delay to use in that instance.

It is interesting to note some other results in this test which was conducted over five years for the top 500 US stocks. The S&P 500 Index was at the 1,210 points level on 2nd March 2005 and was 7.5% lower at 1,120 points on 2nd March 2010. During that time the market had reached a high of 1,565 points and a low of 675 points. The strategy tested, for the above, of the lagging line crossing the cloud produced an overall return of 33% over the five years for all stocks. Sixty percent of the stocks produced a profit with this strategy and forty percent lost. This goes some way to demonstrate the success of the power of the Cloud Chart technique in a falling market. If the market had been trending, this trend following technique would probably have produced even better results. Scrolling through the charts with the trades marked on, one by one, gives a real insight to the effectiveness of the clouds. The chart below is an example some way down the list of top performers with the lagging line crosses of the cloud marked on.

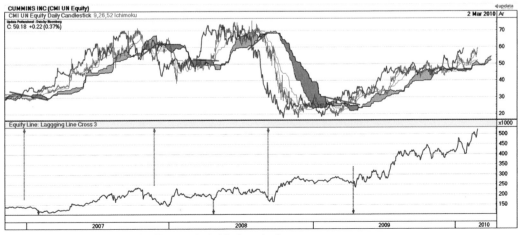

Chart 14-6: Cloud Chart with Lagging Line cross tested for Cummins Inc

A similar optimisation exercise can be conducted on the cloud construction periods of 9, 26 and 52 to see if there is any favoured set of periods for a given universe of instruments. With three variables to optimise this is a considerably bigger set of iterations than the previous signal delay test. For each of the three periods two steps of 3 either side were tested, such that the combinations of any one of; 3,6,9,12,15 and each of; 20,23,26,29,32 and one in the range; 46,49,52, 55, 58 were set. This is a bigger exercise than it looks with hundreds and hundreds of calculations per instrument. The test was conducted on the FTSE 100 Index constituents and took a few hours with a high speed processor computer. To test the cloud periods exhaustively and reach any clear conclusions on which numbers work best would take a very long time and the results of such optimisations would also change over time.

| 1ST PERIOD | | 2ND PERIOD | | 3RD PERIOD | |
|---|---|---|---|---|---|
| No | Freq | No | Freq | No | Freq |
| 3 | 37 | 20 | 31 | 46 | 26 |
| 6 | 17 | 23 | 17 | 49 | 13 |
| 9 | 10 | 26 | 13 | 52 | 17 |
| 12 | 18 | 29 | 18 | 55 | 17 |
| 15 | 20 | 32 | 23 | 58 | 30 |

Figure 14-3: Test results from varying the Cloud Chart construction periods

The table above shows the frequency with which each number came up in the test. It shows that 9, 26 and 52 were generally not the preferred numbers in the test but this isn't really helpful as it is the best combination of all three periods that would be of most interest. Out of the 102 stocks in the test no one combination came up more than four times. While there is no proving that 9, 26 and 52 are the best combination of numbers there is also seemingly little evidence that there is a better combination to use. Results may propagate around a particular combination with more exhaustive tests on different universes, but it appears that the variance of the most profitable period combinations will always be high.

It is also interesting to note the difference between using the optimum periods from the test and the standard 9, 26 and 52 construction periods. The chart on the next page shows that for the optimum periods of 15, 23, 49 for Cairn Energy, the equity line went around five fold over six years as shown in the middle window. Using the standard periods, the equity line went up about 4.5 times as shown in the lower window. We see that nearly all the signals for the two period sets matched, except for an extra buy and sell in autumn 2007 for the standard periods.

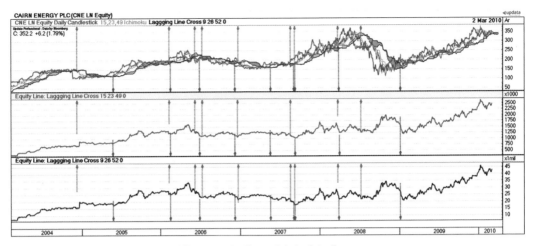

Chart 14-7: Cloud Chart back-tested with different construction periods for Cairn Energy

The main reason for optimising is to find what parameters reduce the number of unprofitable trades. We have already seen that this can be done by keeping the periods constant and using a signal delay. The optimisations will be far quicker with just the signal delay to optimise and it is more akin to reading Cloud Chart signals subjectively. It is hard to prove that 9, 26, and 52 are the best construction periods to use but with the absence of a better combination that can be applied to all instruments, it is best to use the standard periods that we know work well from tests. If you want to trade Cloud Charts as a mechanical system, you should use a signal delay. It also highlights the importance of establishing the normal length of temporary cloud breaches when looking at a chart.

One of the most powerful ways to optimise your trading results for an instrument is to set the chart frame to suit your time horizon and your trading style which might include your preferred trade frequency. This is especially true of intra-day data where you can set your candlesticks to any number of minutes. Here we see a 60 minute chart for crude oil and the equity line trading it long/short on the basis of the lagging line crossing the cloud.

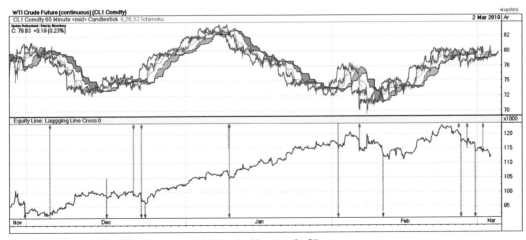

Chart 14-8: 60 minute Cloud Chart back-tested with Lagging Line cross for Oil

The 15 minute chart highlights how trading becomes difficult with prices running sideways.

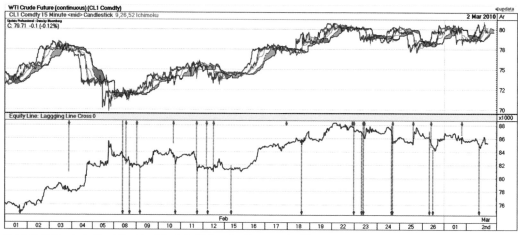

Chart 14-9: 15 minute Cloud Chart back-tested with Lagging Line cross for Oil

## Taking the longer term trend into account

In Chapter 10 we highlighted the importance of taking other time frames into account and we can incorporate this into a Cloud Chart trading system by only taking trades with the longer term trend. Here we see the weekly chart for the S&P 500 Index. In order to 'make the trend your friend' it would be a good strategy to take long trades (daily lagging line crossing up through the cloud) when the weekly lagging line is above the cloud and short trades (daily lagging line crossing below the cloud) when the weekly lagging line is below the cloud.

Chart 14-10: Weekly Cloud Chart for S&P 500 Index highlighting areas for long and short trading

The chart below shows the trades that follow this strategy with a steadily increasing equity curve over the years. You would have avoided counter trend trades and for times when these cloud crosses did occur the equity curve went sideways reflecting being uninvested by not entering a trade.

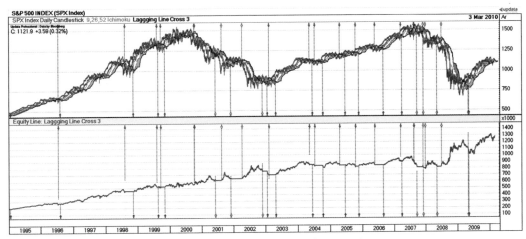

Chart 14-11: Back-test for daily Cloud Chart taking weekly Cloud Chart trend into account

The system works well on currencies as well. For 29 currency rates tested, all made a profit with this strategy over ten years. Here we see the system on the Swedish Krone. A similar trading strategy could be employed with hourly charts using the daily cloud position as their filter, or on 10 minute charts with the hourly as the filter and so on.

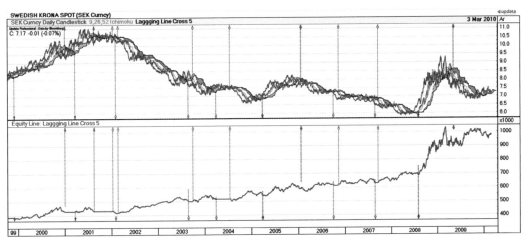

Chart 14-12: Back-test for daily Swedish Krone taking weekly Cloud Chart trend into account

Running this strategy on all of the S&P 500 Index constituents over the last five years taking the weekly cloud positions for each stock into account also produces good results. We use an optimised signal delay as we did in the test conducted earlier in this chapter.

The results were that a profit was made on 430 stocks of the 500 constituents in a sideways market of five years. Here the strategy of not taking counter-trend signals has improved the number of constituents from 60% to 86%. Also the overall profit result improved from 33% to a 79% return across all 500 stocks. Clearly, not taking counter-trend signals improves trading profits dramatically. The Cloud Chart strategy of taking the longer term trend into account produced a return of nearly 80% across the board over a five year period in flat markets.

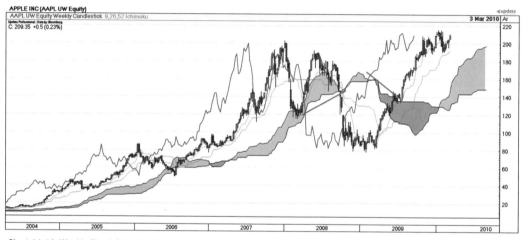

Chart 14-13: Weekly Cloud Chart of Apple

The chart of Apple Inc above shows the weekly chart where we had a year of the stock being bearish. And below we see the log scale daily chart where the strategy of taking the weekly cloud into account was employed. The equity line shows that the trading strategy didn't perform well in 2008, but it would have performed worse had we have taken the buy signals at this time.

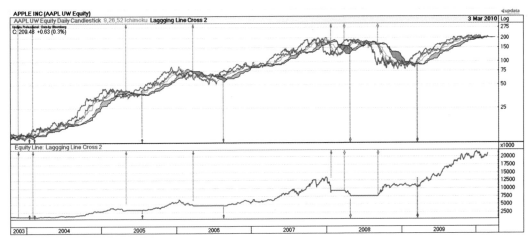

Chart 14-14: Back-test for Apple daily chart taking weekly Cloud Chart trend into account

## Summary points

- Employing a signal delay for reading the cloud cross signals improves trading results
- There is no standard signal delay to use, it is best to optimise per instrument
- Tests on large instrument universes show that the Cloud Chart method works
- There is no evidence to suggest any set of construction periods works best
- Changing the chart time frame for back-testing is a better way of improving results than changing construction periods
- A good overall strategy is to use the longer term chart, such as weekly for daily tests, as a filter for rejecting counter-trend signals
- Virtually any Cloud Chart strategy can be programmed

# Chapter 15 - **Cloud Market Breadth Analysis**

Market Breadth is a long established method of technical analysis which seeks to analyse a group of underlying instruments as a whole. This might be a group of instruments in a sector, such as Banks, or a market index. Market Breadth lines will measure each member instrument in the list to produce a rolling line showing the sum of the criteria for the group. Each member in the list is treated with equal weight which is significant with most indices which will be weighted. For instance, in the UK FTSE 100 Index, the top ten stocks account for around 90% of the weight of the index. A handful of stocks determine most of the movement in the index. With a Market Breadth calculation the smallest weighted stock and the largest weighted stock are treated in the same way. Such a calculation will give a broad picture of the market, hence the term Market Breadth.

The chart below is one of the most famous Market Breadth indicators, the Advance/ Decline Line, often called the A-D Line. This example is calculated on the S&P 500 Index and its 500 constituent stocks. Each day the difference between the number of advancing stocks and the number of declining stocks is added to the cumulative line. If more stocks rise than fall, the line will rise and if more stocks fall than rise, the line will fall. The main purpose of the line is to look for Divergence between the price and the broader picture. Here we see the US stock market in 2009 has recovered around half of its falls in 2008, while the breadth is testing new highs again. This tells us that the recovery is broad based and therefore most stocks are rising.

Chart 15-1: S&P 500 Index with Advance/Decline Line

Calculating Market Breadth does come with a health warning due to constituent changes. The top chart above represents all the constituents over time and will include stocks that are no longer in the index. Some companies will have been taken over and others will have fallen in value, such that they are no longer in the top 500. There will also be new comers, companies that have grown into the top 500 and stocks entering the stock market by way of a public offer. The bottom window, however, represents the changes historically in all the current 500 constituents, some of which weren't in the index a few years ago.

To calculate Market Breadth correctly, you need all of the constituent changes and the histories of the stocks that are no longer in the index, or indeed no longer listed. This data isn't easily available and most technicians will be happy to calculate Market Breadth with the current constituents on the fly. One way to mitigate the effect of constituent changes is to use indices that contain a large number of constituents such as the S&P 500 Index.

Market Breadth indicators are available and can be calculated on just about any criteria. Common breadth tools include; Advance/Decline Spread, Advance/Decline Ratio, Absolute Breadth Index, Thrust Index, Arms Index, McClellan Oscillator, Cumulative Volume Index, New Highs/New Lows and many more. The chart below shows the percentage of stocks above their 52 week moving average on the FTSE 100 Index. From this we can see that the number of stocks above their average is historically high. In the previous market rallies these states were reached and could be maintained for some time. This chart will tend to highlight declines in sentiment first as we saw in 1998, 2000, and 2007.

Chart 15-2: FTSE 100 Index with percentage of stocks above 52 week average

## Bullish Percent

Another effective Market Breadth study is the Bullish Percent indicator which is calculated on the basis of the percentage of stocks in a chosen universe where the last Point and Figure signal way a buy. Because the last signal must either be a buy or a sell, we can tally up the number of bullish stocks. There are a series of rules to reading this line which can be found in Chapter 8 of *The Definitive Guide to Point and Figure* by Jeremy du Plessis.

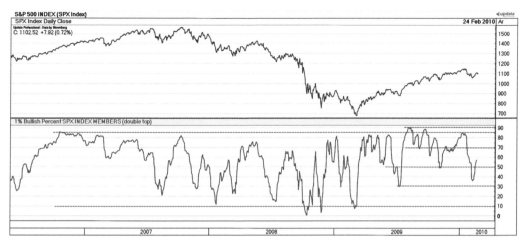

Chart 15-3: S&P 500 Index with Bullish Percent

Market Breadth lines can easily be derived from Cloud Charts for a universe of constituents in a similar way. The bottom window in the chart below shows the number of constituent stocks for the NASDAQ 100 Index where prices are above their daily cloud (blue line) and the number below the cloud (red line). From this we can see times where the market is heavily oversold such as in October 2008 when the percentage of stocks below the cloud was at 90%. We also see times when the market is overbought with stocks above the cloud at 90%. This would help with market timing to ensure you are not buying stocks when the market is overbought.

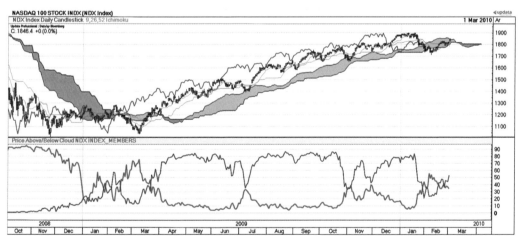

Chart 15-4: NASDAQ 100 Index with number of stock above/below cloud

The chart above only takes account of constituent stocks where prices are above or below the cloud. Consequently the stocks where the current price is in the cloud are not included in the calculation. We can resolve this by keeping a count of each stock's last out of cloud position to arrive at an overall number of stocks that are bullish on price or bearish on price and we see these lines for the chart of the Nikkei 225 Index and its constituent stocks shown on the following page.

Here the sum of the lines can only add up to 100% as each stock's state is either bullish or bearish. Considering the stocks that are in the cloud does give a more complete picture than the previous chart.

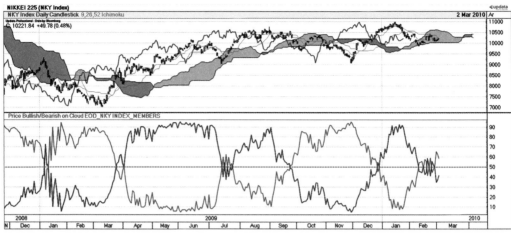

Chart 15-5: Nikkei 225 Index with bullish/bearish stocks based on cloud position

We can take Market Breadth and Cloud Charts a step further by calculating the percentage of stocks where the lagging line is in bullish territory. The chart below shows the percentage of stocks in the S&P 500 Index which are bullish in relation to their clouds. From this we can see the heavily oversold and overbought regions marked at 10% and 90% respectively. At these points, there are less than a tenth of stocks left to join the prevailing state of bearishness or bullishness respectively suggesting an extreme is reached. We can also look for divergence between the Cloud Bullish Percent and the Index of the constituent stocks and we see this occurring in 2007 on the chart which indicates bullishness in the market is becoming less broad based, warning a market top might be near.

Chart 15-6: Daily S&P 500 Index with Cloud Bullish Percent

Cloud Bullish Percent can also be calculated for weekly data and below we see a line, drawn as a smoothed 13 week average, for the number of stocks below their weekly clouds for the S&P 500 Index. We can see how Cloud Bullish Percent was deteriorating before the top of the market in 2000 and 2007. We also see, having just crossed in to bullish territory, how one third of constituents are below their weekly cloud, leaving room for more bullish crosses from here.

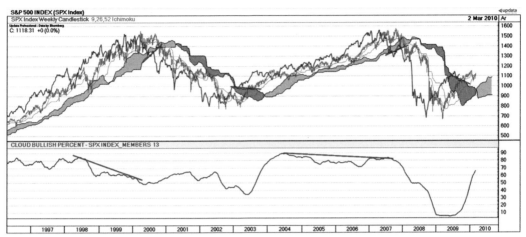

Chart 15-7: Weekly S&P 500 Index with Cloud Bullish Percent

It is also possible to show the breadth for the price and lagging lines together on a chart. Here we see the Cloud Bullish Percent for the lagging line in blue, and for the price line in green, calculated from the Nikkei 225 Index members.

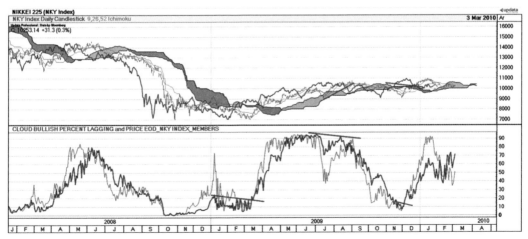

Chart 15-8: Nikkei 225 Index with Cloud Bullish Percent

As we would expect price crosses more often than the lagging line which gives few signals. As on the individual Cloud Charts, Cloud Market Breadth for price does give an early warning that the lagging line is likely to move from the overbought and oversold extremes. On the basis of this chart, the move from the oversold area in early 2009 represented a buying opportunity for Japanese stocks. The divergence several months later, where breadth started falling while prices continued to rise, was an indication that stocks had reached a point of maximum bullishness for a while. The buying opportunity returned at the end of 2009 with breadth rebounding from the oversold extreme before a cloud cross for the Nikkei 225 Index occurred. The latest position on breadth on this chart shows more and more prices crossing below the cloud which suggests the Cloud Bullish Percent based on the lagging line may not reach the overbought extreme.

## Summary points

- Market Breadth measures set criteria of each instrument in a list to give a rolling cumulative total of that criterion
- It is a useful tool for seeing where index weighting disguises the broader picture
- We look for divergence between breadth and price as a sign of change
- Use indices with high numbers of members to mitigate constituent changes effects
- Cloud Bullish Percent shows the percentage of stocks above their clouds
- Cloud Breadth can be calculated on daily or weekly data
- Showing breadth lines for both price and lagging line gives more of a picture of how stocks are interacting with their clouds

# Part 3 Summary

In the first chapter of this final part of the book we saw how standard Technical Analysis techniques and the Cloud Chart method can be integrated. We explored the effect on the charts, from a visual perspective, of altering the 9, 26 and 52 periods for the cloud construction. We saw that these periods need to be varied significantly for Cloud Charts to appear radically different. Shortening the periods does not necessarily provide earlier signals as we might have expected.

Chapter 13 also explored the idea of extending the cloud still further on the basis of an assumption of prices not changing going forward. This extra part of the cloud will recalculate as prices do change. This might provide an edge in understanding potential areas of support and resistance even further out than the 26 bar offset of the normal cloud.

We also looked at a host of standard tools such as moving averages of the cloud midpoints and used these to produce lines such as price distance from the cloud to identify times of price exhaustion. We found that changes in Cloud Width may also be a warning that prices are near a top or a bottom. Cloud Charts can be constructed on relative strength, spreads and even Point and Figure charts by using X and O column midpoints. Cloud Charts can be flipped in just the same way as we explored towards the end of Chapter 4, in order to counter any bull or bear bias you may already have for a given instrument. Last of all in Chapter 13, we looked at Cloud Chart Stop-losses.

Chapter 14 covered back-testing the Cloud Chart technique and deriving trading strategies from the results of some of the ideas tested. We saw how optimising a signal delay on an instrument by instrument basis could improve trading results. We showed that the Cloud Chart technique worked as a trading system overall although it is predominantly a method of analysis with high degree of subjective interpretation as set out in Part 2.

One of the most effective trading strategies is to take signals with the prevailing longer term trend and ignore the counter-trend signals. On the top 500 US stocks this strategy improved the overall profit result from 33% to 79%. The number of stocks where the strategy was loss making was reduced 40% to 14% just by taking the trend of the weekly cloud into consideration and not trading counter-trend.

Finally, in Chapter 15 we looked at using Cloud Charts to create a Market Breadth Indicator, Cloud Bullish Percent. These charts may be used to assess sentiment for stocks across a market as a whole. We saw that for the US stock market, Cloud Bullish Percent provided useful forward insights for turning points in the market. This tool is an ideal way of timing stock purchases and disposals taking account of market conditions. With Cloud Bullish Percent, we know when we need to be underweight and overweight stocks and can distribute and accumulate stocks accordingly.

# Chapter 16 - **Conclusion**

The Cloud Charts technique is among the most valuable new additions to Technical Analysis in decades. Their power is the ability to know the trend on any time horizon instantly. The bullish and bearish zones are unambiguous making the charts the perfect roadmap for your trading and investing. No other technique allows you to swap time frames with no further requirements, such as deciding on an indicator period, and interpret the position of an instrument so quickly and clearly.

Can you rely on Cloud Charts entirely without the use of other Technical Analysis techniques? We have seen throughout the book that your analysis can be strengthened with the use of other techniques. Cloud Charting is a trend following method and as a result will not normally produce clear results at times when prices move sideways and become range bound. At these times you may want to use indicators to trade the range or gain an indication of the likely direction of the breakout of prices from that trading range. Shorter term Cloud Charts should help you trade the range too.

Candlesticks and the patterns derived from them are an integral part of Cloud Charts. Understanding Candlestick techniques will provide an extra dimension to your Cloud Chart Analysis. Point and Figure charts often concur with what Cloud Charts tell us about an instrument, but using Point and Figure price targets with your cloud analysis will provide a powerful addition which you should use.

Should you rely on Cloud Charts for your exit signals? Optimised Stop-losses may serve you better especially for shorter term trading. But, because Cloud Charts are constructed purely from the price, you will get a guaranteed and relatively clear exit signal compared to other techniques.

It is also important not to forget the very basic ideas of price support and resistance. The concept of higher highs and lower lows in price behaviour hold true in Cloud Charts. The basic tenets of Technical Analysis laid down by Charles Dow over a century ago still apply in today's financial markets. The simple rules of price patterns should always be recognised, even when the Cloud Chart becomes congested and difficult to read in sideways markets.

Cloud Chart analysis may appear too subjective to use in practice for the newcomer. The picture is changing all the time with these charts and that is one of their true advantages. Price movement determines the shape of the cloud and this in turn provides areas of support and resistance. Prices can whipsaw in and out of the cloud, and they frequently do, finding support or resistance. This means there is less risk of failed signals than with more precise trend lines. These areas of price support and resistance are projected into the future providing a time based roadmap of dynamic levels where prices need to be at future times for the trend to be maintained. This is a unique aspect of Cloud Charts which no other technique can match.

In addition, you should use multiple time frames with Cloud Charts to build a multi-faceted view of a financial instrument. When conducting an in-depth analysis across a series of time frames, the Cloud Chart is the natural place to want to start. The cloud sets the tone for using other analysis techniques for that time frame. Cloud Charts highlight the nature of trends within trends and potentially conflicting views for different time horizons. At the very least you should always look at a time frame either side of your preferred time horizon. If you are a medium term investor, using daily charts then longer term weekly charts along with shorter term hourly charts, will provide you with a more complete picture. The extra mental bandwidth required to take account of the adjacent time horizons will be minimal with the technique.

Cloud Charts can be applied to other charts such as spreads and relative strength charts. Other indicators can be derived from the charts. You are unlikely to use all of the combinations of charts but there may be one that inspires you to explore things further. There is some indication that tools such as cloud thickness or distance between price and the cloud may provide advance warning of turning points. Cloud Stop-losses have the potential to replace other stop-loss techniques and, as they reflect the price and lagging line in relation to the edge of the cloud, some traders may be happy to use these simpler charts. To give up the complete picture that the cloud provides may be a price worth paying for those that struggle with the noise of the charts. But this should be a last resort.

In this book we have proved with quantitative tests that the Cloud Chart technique is highly profitable as a trading strategy on large universes of instruments. We have seen that these results can be improved further by optimising the time delay in accepting or rejecting a trading signal. We have demonstrated that trading results can be enhanced even further by taking the prevailing trend on the longer term adjacent time frame into account. By rejecting counter-trend signals we arrive at the ultimate strategy for 'making the trend your friend.'

Cloud signals can be scanned for in large instrument universes and the individual bullish and bearish cloud positions can also be tallied to give an overall view of sentiment across a market. These groundbreaking breadth tools using Cloud Charts can provide an early warning of turning points in any given financial market.

## Where next?

Hopefully this book is the beginning of a long journey for you in successfully deploying Cloud Charts for more profitable trading and investing. What started out as a relatively unknown Japanese technique called *Ichimoku* (roughly translated as 'one look') only a few decades ago is now widely used on trading screens around the world. There has been a real shortage of material on the subject and this book is designed to address that. Whether Cloud Charts bring you trading success or not will be less down to this book, which can only get you started, and more down to you practicing using the technique. Cloud Charts are elegantly simple to use, but to gain the true benefit from them you have to start using them when making your trading and investment decisions.

If you are not using Cloud Charts already, there is no time like the present to get started. Download some software right away and experiment with them while this book is still fresh in your mind. You will soon wonder how you ever made trading decisions without them.

The subject of Cloud Charting is still evolving and it is likely to constantly progress. You will find a growing amount of material at cloudcharts.com including more information on all the tools used in this book, trading systems to download, further findings and more groundbreaking ideas. Content includes regular webcasts and practical examples of using Cloud Charts to help you get maximum value from this truly amazing technique.

Finally, the overriding message that you should have gained from reading this book is, that with Cloud Charts, you will always 'make the trend your friend!'

# Appendix 1 - Scanning

It is possible to scan and set alerts for Cloud Chart crosses on either price or the lagging line in Updata software system. This takes a few minutes for very large universes of stocks but may not be possible in other software products so it is covered in this appendix.

The screens below show how you set up the scan criteria. It is important to set criteria for crosses up through the cloud top (bullish) as well as the cloud base at an earlier date. This avoids results being returned where the lagging line entered the cloud from above and ensures we have a full cloud cross.

Figure A-1: Setting up cloud cross criteria

The scan typically runs in under a minute on very large instrument universes and a results screen like the one below is produced.

Figure A-2: Scan results for weekly cloud crosses in last three weeks for S&P 500 stocks

The three charts below are from scrolling the first few results of the scan.

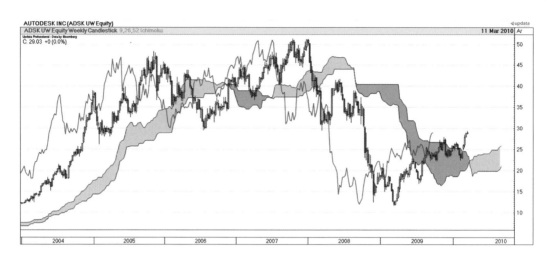

# Bibliography

Boroden, Carolyn, *Fibonacci Trading*,
McGraw Hill, New York, 2008

du Plessis, Jeremy, *The Definitive Guide to Point and Figure*,
Harriman House, Petersfield UK, 2005

du Plessis, Jeremy, *Updata Professional User Manual*, Updata plc, London, 2009

Elliot, Nicole, *Ichimoku Charts*,
Harriman House, Petersfield UK, 2007

*IFTA Journal 2009*, International Federation of Technical Analysts,
Rockville MD, 2009

Kaufman, Perry J, *New Trading Systems and Methods*,
John Wiley & Sons, Hoboken NJ, 2005

Keller, David, *Breakthroughs in Technical Analysis,*
Bloomberg Press, New York, 2007

Morris, Gregory L., *Candlestick Charting Explained*,
McGraw Hill, New York, 1992

Morris, Gregory L., *The Complete Guide to Market Breadth Indicators*,
McGraw Hill, New York, 1992

Murphy, John J., *Technical Analysis of the Financial Markets*,
New York Institute of Finance, New York, 1999

Nison, Steve, *Japanese Candlestick Charting Techniques*,
New York Institute of Finance, New York, 2001

Schabacker, Richard W., *Technical Analysis and Stock Market Profits*,
Harriman House, Petersfield UK, 2005

## Japanese Texts

Hosoda, Goichi, *Ichimoku Kinko Hyo*,
Tokyo, 1968

Sasaki, Hidenobu, *Table of equilibrium at a glance*,
Toshi Radar, Tokyo, 1996

# Other Resources

International Federation of Technical Analysts (IFTA) - www.ifta.org

American Association of Professional Technical Analysts - www.aapta.com

UK Society of Technical Analysts - www.sta-uk.org

## Market Data Services

All of the services below are Updata compatible

Barchart - www.barchart.com

Bloomberg - www.bloomberg.com

CQG - www.cqg.com

DTN IQ Feed - www.dtniq.com

eSignal - www.esignal.com

FutureSource - www.futuresource.com

Google Finance - www.google.com/finance

Interactive Brokers - www.interactivebrokers.com

Montel - www.montelpowernews.com

Morningstar LIM - www.lim.com

Morningstar Tenfore - www.tenfore.com

Mytrack - www.trackdata.com

Reuters - www.reuters.com

Trayport - www.trayport.com

Yahoo! Finance - http:/finance.yahoo.com

Zema - www.ze.com

## Software

Updata Professional - www.updata.co.uk

TraderPro - www.updata.co.uk/private

# Index